HOW CAN MANKIND
FIND THE CHRIST AGAIN?

*The Threefold Shadow-Existence of Our Time
and the New Light of Christ*

Eight lectures delivered in Dornach
December 22, 1918 to January 1, 1919

by
Rudolf Steiner

D1527546

Anthroposophic Press
Hudson, New York

The eight lectures presented here were given in Dornach from Dec. 22, 1918 to Jan. 1, 1919. In the Collected Edition of Rudolf Steiner's works, the volume containing the German texts is entitled, *Wie kann die Menschheit den Christus wiederfinden? Das dreifache Schattendasein unserer Zeit und das neue Christus-Licht.* (Vol. 187 in the Collected Edition) The first lecture was translated by Olin Wannamaker. The remaining lectures were translated by Frances E. Dawson and Gladys Hahn. They were edited for this volume by Gladys Hahn.

First Edition (5 lectures) 1947
Second Edition (Revised with 3 additional lectures) 1984
Reprinted 1988
Copyright © 1984
by Anthroposophic Press

Steiner, Rudolf, 1861–1925.
  How can mankind find the Christ again?

  "Eight lectures delivered in Dornach, December 22, 1918 to January 1, 1919."
  Translation of: Wie kann die Menschheit den Christus wiederfinden?
    1. Anthroposophy—Addresses, essays, lectures.
2. Jesus Christ—Anthroposophical interpretations— Addresses, essays, lectures. I. Hahn, Gladys. II. Title.
BP595.S89413 1984   299'.935   84-326
ISBN 0-88010-078-8
ISBN 0-88010-079-6 (pbk.)

Cover design by Van James
based on the watercolor "Easter" by Rudolf Steiner.

Printed in the United States of America

Table of Contents

iv

Foreword

The quest for an experience of the Christ Forces lives in countless human souls today. Christianity can speak to every human heart and to every level of understanding from child-like devotion to loftiest regions of philosophical life. It was so in history and is still true today.

In hundreds of lectures Rudolf Steiner (1861–1925) has spoken from ever new aspects of this central theme of human life and evolution. The eight lectures published here in a new translation (the last two for the first time) were given during the Christmas season 1918/19 to members of the Anthroposophical Society in Switzerland. Some of the illustrative material was drawn from events of that time at the close of World War I.

As always, Rudolf Steiner spoke freely without using notes. Most of his audience had studied—or were at least familiar with—his written works and the published lecture cycles on the Gospels and related themes. A similar background will be needed for reading *How Can Mankind Find the Christ Again?* Such a background will prepare the reader for challenges and vistas not encountered elsewhere. Steiner's message of the new Christ Light midst the shadow existence of our age speaks to the modern soul in search of a cognitive reach.

Readers who have wrestled with Christ themes on that level and are willing to study this text, consciously kept difficult and low-key, will find here themes spanning the past, present and future of mankind. No other thinker of any age has opened up for modern man such a wealth and depth of insight. As a herald of the new Christ revelation, Rudolf Steiner is practically unknown; so pervasive are the shadows of our age. They obscure even the light of recognition.

For students of Rudolf Steiner's work it should be noted that the last lecture in this series, published here in English for the first time, is unique and frequently noted. Livingness in thinking rather than an amassing and combining of information—this actual shaping of thoughts in an organic way (*Ideegestaltung*)—has been an ever present challenge. This livingness with its formative character is a manifestation of forces newly available to human beings. It has been evident in all of Rudolf Steiner's contributions: in his architectural and sculptural forms and in his unique style of developing thoughts in speaking and writing.

Our activity of thinking, that least observed element of the human soul, today perpetuates habits of past periods in history. Our heritage from Greek, Hebrew, and Roman cultures and the analytic rationalism of Arabism and the Enlightenment—for all their wonder and intellectual achievement—has led to a worldwide cultural impasse. Without a radical change, a transformation in the very way people form their thoughts, without a permeation by that new life embodied in the Christ-Idea—all hope for a renewal of human civilization ends. For readers endowed with a feeling for reality, the urgency of Rudolf Steiner's message will ring true.

George O'Neil
Spring Valley, N.Y., 1984

I

Like two mighty pillars of the spirit have the annual festivals of Christmas and Easter been placed by the Christian world within the course of the year, itself a symbol of the course of human life. On these spiritual pillars standing before the human soul in its contemplation are inscribed the two great mysteries of mankind's physical existence. We must regard them very differently from the way we regard other events in the course of our physical life.

It is true that a supersensible element reaches into this physical life through our sense observation and our intellectual judgments, through the content of our feeling and will. In certain instances it proclaims itself clearly as supersensible —when, for example, Christian feeling undertakes to symbolize it in the festival of Pentecost. With Christmas and Easter, on the other hand, we must look at two events in earthly life that in external appearance would seem perhaps to be completely physical events; and yet, in contrast to all other physical events, they do not—indeed, they cannot by their very nature—present themselves as simply physical events. We can observe human physical life as we observe nature, perceiving with our senses the external manifestation of the spirit. But we can never observe the two boundary events of human life, not even just their physical occurrence, without confronting through physical perception itself their tremendous riddle, their profound mystery. These are the events of birth and death. In the life of Christ Jesus, and in our thoughts of Christmas and Easter reminding us of it, these two events of man's physical life stand before our soul, addressing the Christian heart.

As we contemplate these two great mysteries in their relation to Christmas and Easter, we find illuminating strength for our thinking, a powerful incentive for our willing, and an uplifting of our whole being. They stand there, these two pillars of the spirit, possessing an eternal value.

In the course of human evolution, however, men's capacities have changed for approaching the sublime conceptions of Christmas and Easter. During the early Christian centuries, when the Event of Golgotha had penetrated and shocked many hearts, men gradually found their way to the thought of a Savior dying on Golgotha. In the Crucified One hanging on the Cross they found the idea of redemption. And they gradually formed the powerful imagination of Christ dying on the Cross. But in later times, especially since our modern age began, Christian feeling has adjusted itself to the materialism rising in human evolution and has turned to the picture of the childlike element entering the world as the newborn Jesus.

One may certainly say that a sensitive person will find European Christianity decidedly materialistic from the way it has concentrated in recent centuries upon the Christmas manger. The desire to fondle the infant Jesus—this is not meant in a bad sense—has become trivial in the course of centuries. And many songs about the Jesus Child that today are still considered beautiful, or—as some people would say —charming, seem to us not serious enough for these grave times.

But the conception of Christmas and the conception of Easter are eternal pillars, eternal monuments of the human heart. One can truly say that this age of new spiritual revelations will cast new light upon Christmas, so that gradually it will be experienced in a glorious, new form. It will be our task to hear the call in present world events for a rejuvenation of many old conceptions, the call for a new revelation of the spirit. It will be our task to understand that a new meaning for Christmas is working its way out of world events for the strengthening and uplifting of the human soul.

The birth and death of a human being, however intently we may observe and analyze them, manifest themselves as events happening on the physical plane but in which a spiritual element prevails. No one who reflects earnestly can possibly deny that they give evidence in the way they occur that man is the citizen of a spiritual world. No physical observation of birth and death will ever find anything in what the senses can perceive and the intellect grasp, other than events in which the spirit is directly manifested in the physical. Only these two earthly events appear in this way to the human heart.

For the event of birth, the Christmas event, the human and Christian heart must develop an ever deeper sense of mystery. One may say that men have seldom looked from a high enough level upon the mysterious nature of birth. Seldom, indeed; but then at such moments its tidings speak to the depths of the human soul.

So it is, for instance, with the images associated with that spiritual genius of fifteenth-century Switzerland, Nikolaus von der Flüe.[1] It is related of him—and he himself told it—that before his birth, before he breathed the outer air, he beheld the physical form that he would have after birth and during the course of his life. Also, he beheld before birth the ceremony of his own christening, with the persons who were present and who were then around him in his early childhood. With the exception of one elderly person whom he did not recognize, he knew all these people because he had seen them before he saw the light of the physical world.

However one may view this story, one cannot but see that it points impressively to the mystery of human birth, which is so magnificently symbolized for world history by the Christmas imagery. The story of von der Flüe suggests that there is something connected with our entrance into physical life that only by a very, very thin wall is hidden from our everyday view, a wall so thin that it can be broken through when a karmic situation exists as in the case of Nikolaus von der Flüe. Such moving allusions to the mystery of birth and Christmas still meet us here and there. But one must say that as yet mankind is hardly aware of the fact that birth and death, the two boundary pillars standing there in the physical world, reveal themselves even in their physical appearance as spiritual events that could never occur in the ordinary course of nature, as events in which, on the contrary, divine spiritual Powers actually intervene. This is evident from the fact that both these boundary experiences still remain mysteries, even in their physical manifestation.

The new revelation of the Christ now moves us to contemplate the course of human life—allow me to express it in the following way—as Christ wishes us to contemplate it in the twentieth century. As we try today to grasp the meaning of Christmas, let us recall a saying attributed to Christ Jesus that points truly to the Christmas event: "Except ye become as little children, ye shall not enter the Kingdom of Heaven." "Except ye become as little children": this is certainly not encouraging us to strip away all the mystery of the Christmas conception, and to drag it down to the banality of "dear little Jesus," as many folk songs and other songs have done —the folk songs less than the art songs—during the materialistic development of Christianity. This very saying— "Except ye become as little children, ye shall not enter the Kingdom of Heaven"—impels us to look up to mighty impulses flowing through human evolution. And in our own time, all that is happening in the world can surely be no reason for lapsing into trivial ideas of Christmas, when the human heart is filled with pain, when it must look back upon millions of human beings who have met their death in these last years, must think of countless human beings hungering for food. At this time surely nothing is fitting but to contemplate the mighty thoughts in world history that have impelled and inspired humanity. One can be brought to such thoughts by the saying, "Except ye become as little children." And one can supplement it by these words: "Unless you live your life in the light of this thought, you cannot enter the Kingdom of Heaven."

When a human being enters this world as a child, he has come directly from the spiritual world. What happens in physical life, the procreation and growth of his physical body, is only a covering for the event that cannot be described otherwise than by saying: man's central being leaves the spiritual world. He is born out of the spirit into the body. When the Rosicrucian says "Ex Deo Nascimur," he is speaking of the human being entering the physical world. What first ensheathes him, what makes him a complete physical being here on earth: this is what is referred to by the words "Ex Deo Nascimur." If one would speak of the kernel of the human being, his innermost core of being, one must say: he comes down from the spirit into this physical world. Through what takes place in the physical world—which he is able to observe from spiritual regions before his conception and birth—he is clothed with a physical body, in order that he may have experiences that are only possible in such a body. But he has come, in his central core of being, out of the spiritual world. And he reveals—to one who wants to see things as they really are in this world, who is not blinded by materialistic illusions—he reveals in his very first years by his very nature that he has come out of the spirit. One's experiences with a child, if one has insight, are of such a character that one feels in him the after-effects of his recent life in the spiritual world.

This is the mystery that is indicated by such stories as the one associated with Nikolaus von der Flüe. A trivial view and one strongly influenced by materialistic thinking asserts in its simplicity that a human being develops his ego gradually in the course of his life from birth to death, that his ego becomes more and more clearly manifest and more and more powerful. This is a naïve way of thinking! If one observes the true human ego that comes from the spiritual world into its physical sheath through birth, one speaks quite differently about the entire physical development of the human being. For one knows that as the human being grows physically in his physical body, actually his true ego slowly vanishes into the body, becoming continually less and less manifest. One knows that what develops here in the physical world between birth and death is only a mirrored reflection of spiritual happenings, a dead reflection of a higher life. One is expressing it properly if one says, the entire fullness of a man's being gradually disappears into the body; it becomes more and more invisible. He lives his life here on earth by gradually losing himself in his body. At death he finds himself again in the spirit. That is what one says who knows the facts. Someone ignorant of the facts will declare that a child is incomplete, that his ego gradually develops to greater and greater perfection, growing out of vague subconscious levels of human existence. A knowledge of what the spiritual investigator sees, causes one to speak differently about these things than is done from today's sense-consciousness, enmeshed as it is in external illusions and materialistic feelings.

Thus the human being enters the world as a spiritual being. His bodily nature while he is a child is still undefined; it has as yet laid small claim to his spiritual nature, which is entering into physical existence as if it were falling asleep. This spiritual nature only seems so empty of content to us because we cannot perceive it in ordinary life, just as we cannot perceive the sleeping ego and astral body when they are separated from the physical and etheric bodies. But the fact that we do not perceive a being does not make it less perfect. This is what the human being has to accomplish in regard to his physical body: that he shall bury himself in it more and more deeply, in order to acquire faculties that can only be acquired in this way. His soul and spirit being must lose themselves for a while in physical existence. In order that we may always remember our spiritual origin, in order that we may grow strong in the thought that we have journeyed out of the spirit into the physical world: it is for this reason that the Christmas festival stands there like a mighty pillar of light within the Christian world.

The Christmas imagination must grow ever stronger in the future spiritual evolution of humanity. It will then become powerful again for humanity. Human beings will once more be able to draw strength from it for their physical life; it will remind them in the right way of their spiritual origin. Seldom in our present time does it have so powerful an effect upon human hearts as it will have in the future. For it is a strange fact, but rooted in the very laws of spiritual existence, that what appears in the world to help mankind forward does not appear at once in its ultimate form. It appears first, as it were, tumultuously, as if it were launched prematurely by unlawful spirits of world evolution. We only understand the historical evolution of humanity properly when we realize that truths are not always to be taken up as they first appear. The right moment must also be considered for their entrance into evolution in their true light.

Among various thoughts that have entered into the evolution of modern humanity—inspired, certainly, by the Christ Impulse but appearing at first in premature form—is that of human equality before God and the world, the equality of all men. This is a profoundly Christian conception capable of ever increasing in depth. But it should not have been presented to human hearts in such vague form as it was given by the French Revolution when it first appeared among mankind so tumultuously. We must realize that human life is involved in a process of evolution from birth to death, and that the chief impulses working upon it are distributed in time. Think how it is with the human being as he enters sense-existence: he is filled with the idea of the equality of human nature in all men. We experience the child nature most intensely when we regard the child as permeated through his whole being by this idea. Nothing that creates inequality among men, nothing that organizes men so that they feel different from other men: nothing of all this enters at first into the child's nature. It is all imparted to him in the course of his physical life. Inequality is created by men's physical existence. They come from the spirit equal before God and the world and their fellowmen. This is proclaimed by the mystery of the child.

This mystery is closely related to our understanding of Christmas, which will be made more profound by new Christian revelations. For these will have to do with the new Trinity: the human being, representing all humanity; the forces of Ahriman; and the forces of Lucifer. As one learns how man is placed in world existence in a situation of balance between Ahriman and Lucifer, one comes to understand the real significance of the human being in external physical life.

Most of all, understanding must come about, Christian understanding, for a certain aspect of human life. Someday Christian thought will announce a fact that has already been put forward by some minds since the middle of the nineteenth century—may I say, in stammering accents, but quite distinctly. When one has first grasped the fact that a child enters his earth life with a consciousness of human equality, then one must go on to the fact that as the child becomes a man, unequal powers develop in him—as if from just the fact of being born—powers that are obviously not of this earth. One is then confronting another great mystery of human existence, one that is in direct contrast to the idea of equality. To see into this mystery will help one to form a true picture of mankind—something that already at this present moment in time has become earnestly necessary for the future evolution of the human soul. One faces the startling fact that human beings begin to differ from one another while they are growing out of childhood, by reason of something that obviously is born in them, something in their blood: that is, their various gifts and capacities.

One meets the question of gifts and capacities that create such inequality among men in connection with the thought of Christmas. Future Christmas festivals will point to the origin of this vast difference throughout the world in human capacities, talents, even genius. A person will only attain balance in his life when he has learnt to know the origin of certain capacities that are distinguishing him from other men. The light of Christmas, of the Christmas candles, must provide an explanation for evolving humanity. It must answer the question: Do individuals suffer injustice between birth and death from the way the universe is ordered? What is the truth about capacities and talents?

Dear friends, many things will be seen in a different light when mankind has become permeated by the new Christian feeling. Particularly, it will be understood why an esoteric knowledge of the Old Testament included special insight into the nature of prophecy. Who were those prophets who appear in the Old Testament? They were individuals who had been sanctified by Jahve and authorized by Him to use special spiritual gifts that reached far beyond those of ordinary men. Jahve had first to sanctify those capacities that are born to men through the blood. We know that Jahve influences human beings in the time between their falling asleep and waking; He does not work in their conscious life. Every true believer of the Old Testament said in his heart: The capacities and talents that differentiate men, rising to the level of genius in the case of a prophet, are indeed born with the individual. But they are not used by him beneficently unless he sinks in sleep into the realm where Jahve guides his soul impulses. Jahve, active from the spiritual world, transforms his talents; otherwise they would only be physical, only part of his bodily organism.

We point here to the deep mystery of an Old Testament conception. But this must die away, including the belief in the nature of a prophet. New conceptions must enter the evolution of world history for the salvation of mankind. The talent that the ancient Hebrew believed was sanctified by Jahve during unconscious sleep must now in this modern age be sanctified by the human being himself when he is awake and in a state of clear consciousness. But he can only do this if he knows that all natural gifts, capacities, talents, even genius, are luciferic endowments, that they work luciferically in the world unless they are permeated and sanctified by all that enters the world as the Christ Impulse. One touches upon a tremendously important mystery in the evolution of modern humanity if one grasps this central fact of the new Christmas thoughts. The Christ must be so felt, so understood that a human being can now stand before Him as a New Testament believer and say: In spite of my childhood sense of equality, I have been endowed with various capacities and gifts. But they can only contribute to the salvation of mankind if I dedicate them to the service of Christ Jesus, if I permeate my whole nature with the Christ, so that they may be freed from the grasp of Lucifer.

A heart permeated by the Christ tears away from Lucifer what otherwise works luciferically in human physical existence. This must be the powerful thought that will pervade the future evolution of the human soul. It is the new Christmas thought, the new annunciation of Christ's activity in our souls, transforming the luciferic influence. Lucifer's power in us is not due to our having come out of the spiritual world, but to the fact that we are clothed by a physical body permeated by blood. We have our talents through heredity. Our individual capacities come to us through the luciferic stream of heredity. They must be mastered and put to use during physical life not through inspirations we receive from Jahve during sleep, but through the Christ Impulse that we can feel working within us in our fully conscious life.

"Oh, Christian," says the new Christianity, "turn your thoughts to Christmas! lay upon the Christmas altar all the differentiation you have received through your blood! sanctify your capacities, gifts, genius as you behold them illuminated by the light coming from the Christmas tree!"

The new revelation of the spirit must speak a new language, and we must not be dull and unheeding as it addresses us in this extremely serious time. If we remain receptive, then we will find the power that mankind must find for the great tasks that will confront us in this very age. We must experience the meaning of Christmas in all its gravity. Today we must realize in clear waking consciousness what the Christ was really saying when He spoke those words, "Except ye become as little children, ye cannot enter the Kingdom of Heaven." The sense of equality that is natural to a child is not—if we regard him properly—proved false by these words. For the Child Whose birth we commemorate on Christmas Eve reveals ever new thoughts to mankind in the course of our evolution. He now proclaims that we must place all the distinguishing capacities we possess within the light of the Christ who ensouled this Child. All that our different talents achieve must be brought to the altar of this Child.

Perhaps, stirred by the earnestness of this Christmas thought, you will now ask, "How am I to experience the Christ Impulse in my own soul?" This question is often a burden in men's hearts.

Dear friends, what we may call the Christ Impulse does not become rooted in our souls in a moment, suddenly and

11

tempestuously. It has taken root differently at different periods of evolution. In our present time a human being must take up in full, clear waking consciousness the cosmic truths that have been imparted stammeringly by our anthroposophically oriented spiritual science. As these truths are made known and as he comes to understand them, they will awaken in him the assurance that a new revelation, the new Christ Impulse for this age, has been brought to him. He will perceive the new Impulse if only he is attentive.

Try—in a truly lively way such as is appropriate for this age—to take into yourselves the spiritual thoughts of the cosmic Powers; try to take them up not merely as a teaching, or a theory, but so that they move your souls to their very depths and warm them, illuminate them, permeate them, so that you carry the thoughts living within you! Try to feel them so intensely that they seem to enter your soul by way of your body and change the body itself. Try to strip away from them all abstractions, all theory. Try to realize that they are true nourishment for the soul; they are not just thoughts, they are spiritual life coming from the spiritual world.

Enter into the most intimate inner union with these truths and you will observe three things. First you will observe that gradually—however they may be expressed—they eradicate from your soul something that usually appears so obviously in human beings in this age of the consciousness soul: self-seeking. When you begin to notice that they kill egotism and disarm self-seeking, then you will have perceived the Christ-permeated character of the thoughts of our anthroposophical spiritual science.

Secondly, observe the moment that untruthfulness approaches you, untruthfulness in any form, either when you yourself are tempted to be careless about the truth or when the falseness approaches you from the outside. If at such a moment you can also observe that immediately there is an impulse moving within you, warning you, pointing to the truth, admonishing you and impelling you to hold fast to the truth, wanting to prevent falsehood from entering your life—in contrast to ordinary present-day life, so much inclined to sham—then you are again experiencing the living Christ Impulse. No one will find it easy to lie, or to be casual about sham and pretence, in the presence of the spiritual thoughts of anthroposophy. A sign pointing the way to a sense for truth—apart from all other aspects of understanding: this you will find in the thoughts of the new revelation of the Christ. When you have reached the point where you do not seek a merely theoretical understanding of spiritual science, as is sought for any other science, but where the thoughts so penetrate you that you say to yourself, "Now that these thoughts are united with my soul, it is as if a Power of conscience stood beside me admonishing me, directing me toward the truth": then you will have found the second aspect of the Christ Impulse.

In the third place, when you feel that something streams from these thoughts even down into your body, but especially into your soul, working to overcome illness, making you healthy and strong, when you sense the rejuvenating, invigorating power of these thoughts, the adversaries of illness: then you will have experienced the third aspect of the Christ Impulse. This is the goal toward which mankind strives through the new wisdom, in the new spirit: to find in the spirit itself the power to overcome egotism and the falseness of life, to overcome self-seeking through love, the sham of life through truth, illness through health-giving thoughts that put us into immediate accord with the harmonies of the universe, because they flow from the harmonies of the universe.

Not all these things can be attained at the present time, for man carries an ancient heritage around with him! There is a foolish lack of understanding, for instance, when such a backstairs politician as Christian Science twists into a carica-

13

ture the thought of the healing power of the spirit. Even though, due to our ancient heritage, our thinking is not yet sufficiently powerful to accomplish what we long to accomplish—perhaps from a selfish motive—nevertheless thought does possess healing power. But in regard to such things people's ideas are always distorted. Someone who understands may tell you that certain thoughts give you health, and then he is suddenly stricken with this or that illness. It is indeed due to that ancient heritage that we cannot today be relieved of all illness merely by the power of our thought. But are you able to say what illness you would have had if you had not possessed these thoughts? Can you say that you could have passed your life in your present state of health if you had not had these thoughts? Can you prove that a person who has interested himself in our spiritual science and then has died at forty-five years of age, would without these thoughts not have died at age forty-two or age forty? People think the wrong way around! They concern themselves with what their karma cannot bestow upon them and pay no attention to what their karma does bestow upon them. If—in spite of every contradiction in the external world—you will watch and observe through the power of inner trust that you have gained from an intimate acquaintance with the thoughts of spiritual science, you will perceive the healing power that is penetrating even your physical body, the health-giving, freshening, rejuvenating force that is the third element which Christ the Healer brings with His continuous revelations to the human soul.

We wanted to enter more deeply into the thought of Christmas which is so closely related to the mystery of human birth. We wanted to bring in brief outline what is revealed to us today from the spirit as a continuation of the thought of Christmas. We can feel that it gives strength and support to our lives. We can feel that it places us, no matter what happens, in the midst of the impulses of cosmic evolution. We

14

can feel ourselves united with those divine impulses; we can understand them and draw power for our will from this understanding, and light for our life of thought. Humanity is evolving—it would be wrong to deny it. Our only right course is to go forward with this evolution.

And Christ has declared: "I am with you always, even to the end of the world." This is not just a phrase, it is truth. Christ has not only revealed Himself in the Gospels; Christ is with us; He reveals Himself continually. We must have ears to hear what He is ever newly revealing in this modern age. Weakness will overcome us if we have no faith in these new revelations; but strength will be ours if we have such faith.

Strength will indeed come to us if we accept the new revelations, even if they speak to us from life's seemingly contradictory suffering and misfortune. We journey as individual souls through repeated earth-lives during which our destiny comes to fulfillment. Even this thought, which enables us to sense the spiritual working behind external physical life, even this we can only accept if we take into ourselves in a truly Christian sense the revelations that follow one another. The Christian in this age, the true Christian, when he stands before the candles on the Christmas tree, should begin to work with the strengthening thoughts that can now come to him from the new cosmic revelations, bringing power to his will and illumination to his thinking. And his feeling should support the power and light of his thought in the course of the Christian year, to help him approach that other thought that points to the mystery of death: the Easter thought, which brings the final experience of human earthly existence before our souls as a spiritual experience. We will feel the Christ more and more livingly as we are able to place our own existence in the right relation to His life. The Rosicrucian of the Middle Ages, uniting his thought with Christianity, declared: Ex Deo Nascimur; in Christo Morimur; Per Spiritum Sanctum Reviviscimus. Out of the Divine we have been born, if we think of ourselves as human beings here on earth. In Christ we die. In the Holy Spirit we shall be awakened again. This all pertains to our life, our individual human life. If we look away from our own life to the life of Christ, then we see our life as mirrored reflection. Out of the Divine we are born; in Christ we die; in the Holy Spirit we shall be awakened again. This saying is true of the Christ living in our midst as our first-born Brother. We can so affirm it that we feel it to be the Christ-truth raying forth from Him and reflected in our human nature. Out of the Spirit was He begotten—as it stands in the Gospel of Luke, represented by the symbol of the descending dove—out of the Spirit was He begotten; in the human body He died; in the Divine will He rise again.

We can only perceive eternal truths in the right way if we see them in their contemporary reflection—not in a single, absolute, abstract form—and if we feel ourselves not as abstract humanity but as live, individual human beings whose duty is to think and act in harmony with the time in which we live. Then we will try to understand the Christ, who is with us "always, even to the end of the world," to understand Him in His contemporary language as He teaches and enlightens and empowers us through the thought of Christmas. We will want to take the Christ into ourselves in His new language. We must become intimately related to Him. Then we will be able to fulfill in ourselves His true mission on this earth and beyond death. In each epoch human beings must take the Christ into themselves in their own way. This has been people's feeling when they have beheld in the right way the two great pillars of the spirit, Christmas and Easter.

That profound German mystic, Angelus Silesius,[2] expressed it in this way:

"Should Christ a thousand times in Bethlehem be born
And not in thee, then wert thou still forlorn."

16

And, contemplating Easter, he wrote:

"The cross of Golgotha must be upraised in thee
Ere from thy sin its power shall make thee free."

Truly, the Christ must live within us. We are not human beings in some abstract sense, we are human beings of a definite epoch, and the Christ must be born within us in our epoch in accordance with His words. We must endeavor to bring the Christ to birth within us, for our strengthening, for our illumination. As He has remained with us until now, as He will remain with mankind throughout all ages, even to the end of earthly time, so He wills now to be born in our souls. If we try to experience the birth of Christ within us in this epoch, as it becomes a light and a power in our soul—the eternal Light and eternal Power entering into time—then we perceive in the right way the historical birth of Christ in Bethlehem and its image in our own souls.

"Should Christ a thousand times in Bethlehem be born
And not in thee, then wert thou still forlorn."

As He creates the impulse in our hearts today to contemplate His birth—His birth in the course of human events, His birth in our individual souls—so we deepen the thought of Christmas within us. And so let us look toward that "night of consecration" (Weihenacht), which we should feel is bringing a new strength and a new illumination to mankind, to help them to endure the many evils and sorrows they have had to suffer and will still have to suffer.

"My Kingdom," Christ said, "is not of this world." It is a saying that challenges us, if we regard His birth in the right way, to find in our own souls the path to His Kingdom where He will give us strength and light for our darkness and helplessness, through the impulses coming from the world of which He Himself spoke, which His appearance at Christmas will always proclaim. "My Kingdom is not of this world." But He has brought His Kingdom into this

17

world, so that we may always find strength, comfort, confidence, and hope bestowed upon us in all the circumstances of life, if only we will come to Him, taking His words to heart, words such as these:

"Except ye become as little children, ye shall not enter the Kingdom of Heaven."

II

The mood of the present time is not likely, perhaps, to create in many people that depth of inner feeling of which legends and sagas speak when they refer to the Christmas Holy Nights, when the soul that is prepared for it is able to have some experience of the spiritual world. You know one such impressive legend from the performances given here, that of Olaf Åsteson. Many similar things point to Christmas time in the same way.

It is clear, not only to a more thoughtful student of the human heart, but to anyone who observes in the external world the general spirit of our time, that a Christmas mood, a Christmas impulse, must now be sought anew by mankind. What lives in the celebration of Christmas, in the thought of Christmas, must take hold of the human soul in a new way. Just think, dear friends—in order to realize the broader aspects of our contemporary religious and spiritual mood— how little inclination there is at this time to contemplate the Christ as such, to direct the eyes of the soul to Him.

People often believe they are speaking about the Christ, and yet you will find they have made hardly any distinction between Christ and God the Father except in name. While it is true that for many believers the Christ still stands at the center of their religious creed and that beside Him all else of a divine nature loses its luster, nevertheless we have seen for some time now the rise of a theology that has really lost the Christ, that speaks of a God in general even when Christ is meant. The specific quality that is essential when the human heart looks up to Christ needs to be found again.

And perhaps the most worthy celebration of the Christmas Festival at this time is actually to inscribe in our souls how mankind can find the Christ again. Many historical facts of the evolution of mankind will first have to be considered—in the spiritual scientific sense—if a true impulse is to be reawakened that will lead human souls to Christ.

The Christmas Festival can not only remind us, as is intended, of the entrance of Jesus into earth life, but it can also point to the birth of Christianity itself, the entrance of Christianity into the course of earth evolution. And so let us today direct our spiritual vision primarily to what might be called the Christmas of Christianity itself, the entrance, the birth, of Christianity within the sphere of the earth. The external facts are known, of course, but our knowledge of them needs to be intensified.

Christianity came into the world in the person of Christ Jesus, into the midst of the adherents of the Old Testament. We can observe the phenomena that occurred among these people when Christianity was born. We see how they were externally divided into two separate currents, that of the Pharisees and that of the Sadducees. It is necessary to view all these things henceforth in a new light. When we consider the general course of development of an individual or of humanity itself—indeed, the course of the entire earth—this will become increasingly clear to us if we conceive it as a continual balancing between luciferic and ahrimanic forces. But that is merely the designation we use; there has always existed among the deeper natures of humanity a consciousness of the actual existence of Lucifer and Ahriman and of the condition of balance between them. Fundamentally, the contrast of the Pharisaic element and the Sadducean element in the ancient Hebrew evolution was nothing else than the contrast of ahrimanic and luciferic elements. Jesus, coming into external earth life, entered the balancing

20

stream. He entered earthly existence at that place for which the most important designation up to the time of the Mystery of Golgotha was that Solomon's Temple had been built there. In a certain sense we can only understand the nature of Solomon's Temple if we are able to perceive it in contrast to the Christianity then being born. It is well-known how quickly after Christianity came into being Solomon's Temple was destroyed, so far as external existence is concerned. This memorial of the earlier evolution out of which the spirituality of Christianity arose was destined to exist no longer at the place from which that spirituality streamed forth. The nature of Solomon's Temple and the nature of Christianity present a strong contrast. Solomon's Temple embraced in marvelous, magnificent, sometimes gigantic symbols all that was contained in the world conception of the Old Testament. It was an image of the entire universe so far as this could be represented by the ancient world conception, in its conformity to law, in its inner structure, in its permeation by divine-spiritual beings. It was nonetheless an image of the universe that in a certain sense and in one direction was extraordinarily one-sided. That is to say, the Temple was a spatial image of the universe, an image that made use of spatial forms and spatial relations to express the mysteries of the universe. But for those who viewed it in the spirit of the Old Testament, its symbolism was endowed with life.

We see, on the one hand, in the Judaism of the Pharisees and Sadducees, the externalization of what had been given to humanity through the Old Testament; on the other hand, we see in the symbolism of Solomon's Temple the means of deepening the life of Old Testament humanity. It might be said that what has flowed into the entire Old Testament revelation came to expression in these two directions: one outward, exoteric, in the Judaism of the Pharisees and Sadducees; the other esoteric, through what was represented in the mysterious symbols of Solomon's Temple. And from this exotericism and esotericism sprang what became Christianity.

This Christianity was at first, at the time of its birth, unknown to the world at large, to that world in which lived the spirituality of the humanity of that time, namely, the Greek world. Within the expanding Roman empire in which the Mystery of Golgotha was being prepared through the birth of Jesus, it was not known what a momentous Event had taken place among the Jewish people. Nothing was known of the significant Event that constitutes the meaning of the earth. Nevertheless, although the humanity of that time allowed it to pass unnoticed outwardly, the most sublime Event of our earth evolution, inwardly the Christianity that was coming into being was connected with what was then considered the whole world.

In what ways, dear friends, was it connected? The meaning that Christmas conceals is revealed later in the Easter conception. What then is the important aspect of Easter that really intensifies the meaning of Christmas? It is the contemplation of the Savior of mankind Who died on the cross: the cross with the dead God. The intention and the deed originated in humanity: to put to death the God Who had appeared in their midst. The profound magnitude, the full power, of this thought should again enter into human souls. Contemplation of the deed by which the God Who appeared on earth was killed by men: this should be put into language by which it can be understood. Let us try to do this, at least from one point of view.

When we look upon the Mystery of Golgotha, we find it to be a great world-historical confluence of spiritual streams that had been present in the ancient Mysteries. (You know this from my book, *Christianity as Mystical Fact*.) What had taken place in the ancient Mysteries as the sacrificial rite, the rite of initiation, what had taken place in the temple with, one might say, limited importance, was now set out on the great stage of world history; it now took place in the realm of our entire earth existence. In a certain sense, the initiation of humanity itself was brought out of the temples and presented as historical event before the whole world.

Now let us ask: what were the thoughts of someone permitted to take part in the initiation rites of the ancient Mysteries—when these still possessed their true significance? Through his preparatory instruction such a person knew with certainty that what is directly apparent in the external world of the senses, and what can be comprehended by the human intellect, is a world of mere phenomena, a world of appearance. He knew that what a human being experiences immediately in his environment during his waking hours between birth and death is only the outer view, the phenomenal display, of an inner reality, and that in ordinary life this inner reality is concealed. In the Mystery rite itself such a person sought true reality in what streamed to him, as it were, from the depths of existence, in what could be drawn out and separated from the merely phenomenal, illusory existence. Someone who took part in the ancient Mysteries could always say to himself: When I walk through the world and see external nature, it is illusion. When I experience this or that in the world, it is illusion. When I do any kind of work for the world, it is illusion. But when I am permitted to take part in the holy acts of the Mysteries in the Temple, then something happens that is truth, not illusion. Something is drawn forth, so to speak, out of the illusory existence of the world and transformed into a sacramental act; and this act contains exact truth in contrast to the illusion.

If we wish to be quite clear concerning this view of the Mysteries, we must compare it to the view prevailing today in our materialistic age. We must understand that all that is called reality today in this age of materialism was regarded as illusion in the conceptions belonging to the Mysteries;

while, for example, the sacramental act performed as the initiation rite, which most people today consider "fantastic," was esteemed by those acquainted with the Mysteries as the only reality in life. Such an act, therefore, was not performed at random, but at certain times when it was believed that something of the true nature of things might push through the phenomena of outer life and, as it were, be captured through the act. It has often been mentioned that one such important rite consisted in showing the sacrifice of the God, the death of the God, and His resurrection after three days. This pointed to the fact that to someone who penetrates more deeply into the external world, death can reveal the true nature of this world, that reality must be sought beyond death.

Think of all this entering human souls from the content of the Mysteries at the beginning of our Christian era, expressing the most important fact in world phenomena! Someone in that era pondering on the course of our earth evolution would have been able to say: "In ancient times it was possible for man to learn something about the divine-spiritual world through atavistic initiation science. It was formerly revealed to man out of earth evolution itself. That time is now past. The time has come when nothing more can be drawn from the content of this world to guide us to the divine-spiritual world. This world has lost its divine-spiritual life." That is what such a soul would have said. Where must one look for the meaning of evolution for earth-humanity? Where was the real meaning of the earth at the time when Christianity came into being? Where was the expression of what was willed in man's innermost being at that time? At Golgotha on the cross. It was Death! What formerly had gushed forth from earth evolution for human salvation, was itself dead. To the soul that penetrated more deeply into cosmic reality, an earth impulse, the most profound of all earth impulses, was given at the time of the birth of Christianity, in the contemplation of the dead God.

Only when experienced in this way does the full magnitude appear of the matter with which we are here concerned. The ancient world conception, the ancient world-wisdom had flowed into Solomon's Temple; but it no longer held anything of what had made it great. Something new had to enter world evolution. And so in the course of time the destruction of Solomon's Temple and the rise, the birth, of Christianity exactly coincided. Solomon's Temple: a spatial symbolic image of the content of the cosmos; Christianity, comprehended as a time-phenomenon: a new image of the cosmos. Christianity is not something that appears as a spatial image, as in the case of Solomon's Temple; one only understands Christianity if one grasps it in images of *time*. One must see that earth evolution proceeded as far as the Mystery of Golgotha; then the Mystery of Golgotha intervened; then, through the Christ pouring Himself into humanity, evolution moves on in this way or that. Its deeper content is not to be equated in the remotest degree with anything appearing in spatial images, not even in the gigantic, magnificent spatial images of Solomon's Temple. Nevertheless, Solomon's Temple, as also the inner aspect of Pharisaic and Sadducean life, contained the soul of the world consciousness of that time. The soul of the world consciousness two thousands years ago was to be found in Old Testament Judaism. Into this soul was laid the seed of Christianity, a new seed that, while growing out of all that may be expressed in space, can only be expressed in time. The *becoming* following the existing: that is the inner relation of Christianity that was then being born to the soul element of the world of that time, to Judaism that was embodied in Solomon's Temple, which later collapsed. Christianity was born into the *soul* of ancient Judaism.

As Christianity sought the *soul* in Judaism, so it sought the *spirit* in Hellenism. The Gospels themselves, as transmitted to the world (I refer only to what has been handed down), have in the main passed through the Greek spirit. The thoughts through which the world could think Christianity are the spiritual wisdom of Greece. The first apologia of the Church Fathers appeared in the Greek tongue. Just as Christianity was born into the soul that for the humanity of that time lived in Judaism, so it was born into the spirit provided by Hellenism.

Romanism furnished the *body*. It was Romanism that at that time could provide an external organization for concepts of empire. Judaism soul, Hellenism spirit, Romanism body—body, of course, in the sense that the social structure of humanity is body. Romanism is in reality the forming of external inclinations and institutions; the thoughts concerning external institutions live within them. It is the corporeal element in historical existence, the corporeal element in historical development. Just as Christianity was born into the soul of Judaism and into the spirit of Hellenism, so it was born into the body of the Roman Empire. Superficial people even think that everything contained in Christianity can be explained out of Judaism, Hellenism and Romanism. In the same way, indeed, that materialistic natural scientists believe that everything in a human being is inherited from parents, grandparents, etc., ignoring the fact that the soul comes from spiritual regions and only puts on the body as a garment: so these superficial people like to say that Christianity consists of what in actual fact it has only put on as an outer garment. The essence of Christianity entered the world, of course, with Christ Jesus Himself; but this Christianity was born into the Jewish soul, into the Greek spirit, and into the body of the Roman Empire. That, in a sense, is the birth of Christianity itself, viewed in the light of Christmas thought.

It is important not to accept these facts as mere external theories, but to relate them deeply to our thought of Christmas, to learn what their significance really is in relation to the newborn Impulse that is now entering world evolution with the Spirits of Personality—as I explained here recently.[3] Indeed, dear friends, anything new that purposes to enter into the course of world evolution must first struggle through what remains of the old. This is precisely the mystery of world-becoming, that on the one hand there is a normal, progressive evolution; on the other hand, retarded luciferic and ahrimanic forces interfere with it and modify it, but also in a certain sense support it as it advances. I have often called attention to the fact that we cannot escape this ahrimanic-luciferic force; we must look straight at it calmly, and face it consciously. On no account must we simply submit to these things unconsciously. From world impulses shadows remain behind that continue to have an effect even after something new has come into existence; but their luciferic and ahrimanic character must be recognized. This ahrimanic-luciferic element must accompany evolution, but it must not be accepted in an absolute sense; its luciferic-ahrimanic character must be perceived. Something shadow-like has remained behind from Solomon's Temple, something shadow-like also from Hellenism, and something shadow-like from the Roman Empire. Nearly two thousand years ago it was self-evident that from these three—soul, spirit, and body—Christianity was born. But soul, spirit, and body could not immediately disappear; they remained in a certain way as after-effects. Now is the time when this fact must be clearly understood and when the completely unique character of the Christ Impulse itself must be realized.

A shadow remains behind from the most important extract of the esoteric Old Testament, from the Mystery of Solomon's Temple; a shadow remains from Hellenism; also one from the Roman Empire. We must learn to distinguish the shadows from the light. It will be mankind's task from this present time into the immediate future to differentiate between the shadows and the light in the right way.

We see the shadow of the Roman Empire in Roman Catholicism. This is not Christianity; it is the shadow of the ancient Roman Empire into which Christianity had to be born. In its forms there continues to live what had to be built up at that time as a framework for Christianity. But we must learn—humanity must learn—to distinguish the shadow of the old Roman Empire from Christianity. The essence of Christianity is not to be found in the organization of the Catholic Church, or indeed of any of the Christian churches. One sees in their hierarchical aspect what existed and developed in the Roman Empire from Romulus to the Emperor Augustus. The illusion arises only because Christianity was born into this body.

In this sense Solomon's Temple has also remained as a shadow. The Mysteries of Solomon's Temple have—with a few exceptions—been completely absorbed into the Masonic and other secret societies of the present time. As the Roman Church is the shadow of the ancient Roman Empire, so what continues to exist in these societies—however strongly they assert to the contrary, even to the extent of excluding Jews—is the shadow of ancient Judaism, the shadow of the esoteric Jehovah-worship. Again the shadow must be distinguished from the light. Just as the shadow expressed in the perpetuation of the Roman Empire in the Catholic Church, in the churches generally, must be distinguished from the light shining in Christianity, so the element into which Christianity had to be born as soul must be distinguished from the shadow that continues to work in societies founded on symbolism that is reminiscent of Solomon's Temple.

These things must be recognized. They must be looked at in the right way. And they must be illuminated in our time by the new revelations of which we have been speaking during these days.

The Greek spirit into which Christianity had to be born—in spite of all the beauty of Hellenism, in spite of its esthetic and other important content, in spite of the influence it has upon us—has left its shadow as the modern world conception of the cultured humanity that has brought this fearful catastrophe[4] upon mankind. When Hellenism existed with its world conception, it was something different. Everything, dear friends, is right in its own time. If something is taken in an absolute sense, and carried on after it has become antiquated, it then becomes the shadow of itself. And the shadow is not the light; it may change suddenly into the opposite of the real thing. Aristotelianism still shows something of the greatness of ancient Greece. Aristotle in modern raiment is materialism. Christianity was born into the Jewish soul, the Greek spirit, the Roman body; but the three have left their shadows behind. The challenge sounds through our time, like the call of an angel's trumpet, to perceive the true facts, to look through the shadows to the light.

Truly, anyone who ponders over this present moment in time, who considers impartially, without prejudice, what has brought about the fearful, distressing events of recent years, surely cannot help wondering whether some sort of light can be sought that would shine into the darknesses of earth in a different way from those lights which most people still wish to regard as the only ones. One should find the will to look for a way through the shadows to the light. For the shadows will assert themselves. They will become effective through people who perhaps have endured little themselves of the great suffering of humanity at the present time, who have no sympathy, or very little, for the terrible agony that has flashed through the world, agony that is itself proof that

29

many of the thoughts which have appeared were destined to be shipwrecked. One who tries to examine with deeper understanding what is really not difficult to see today, one who has the resolute will to look without prejudice at what is happening today among men, will feel an impulse to seek the light. He should attach some importance to this impulse in his soul, not listen to those who—depending on the place they occupy—wish only to defend one of the ancient shadows, but listen to his own soul; it will speak clearly enough if only he does not let its voice drown under the external assertions of the shadows.

If today one looks compassionately at what has happened, what is happening, and what will happen, one will be able to see a strange figure standing before men: a distortion of the truly human form, in garments woven of shadows, a figure uniting in itself in its thoughts, sensations, feelings, and will-impulses what has put humanity on a wrong track and gives every promise of taking it farther on the wrong track. Deep within what is happening outwardly dwell those three shadow-thoughts that have been described.

Whoever learns to see that figure in garments woven of shadows, has prepared himself in the right way to look at something else: to look at the tree that can illuminate even today's darkness with its lights. Whoever is pure in heart and does not allow himself to be misled by the threefold shadow-existence—antiquated symbolism, antiquated ecclesiasticism, antiquated materialistic science—will see what wills to shine in the darkness as a real Christmas tree, and lying beneath it the Christ-Jesus Child, illuminated anew by the Christmas light. This is the real aim of our anthroposophically-oriented science of the spirit: to seek the Christmas light, so that the Jesus Child, Who entered the world first to work and then to be understood, may gradually be understood; to illuminate in a modest way the greatest of all events in earth existence. This is the goal of our anthroposophical spiritual science within the religious currents of humanity. People will not understand the light that this spiritual science wants to recognize as its Christmas light unless they have the will really to penetrate the three-fold shadow-existence of our time. The times are serious. And whoever lacks the will to take them seriously will perhaps not be able in this incarnation to see what should truly be perceptible at this time to every human being of good will, there for the healing of the many wounds that otherwise mankind will still have to suffer. People of good will should take notice of what may be seen when the anthroposophical science of the spirit enkindles the Christmas light. The light is truly small, and he who professes it remains humble. He does not wish to extol it to the world as something special, for he knows that now it appears small and insignificant, and many men and many generations must still come, to help what now burns dimly to become brighter. But even though the light is weak, it shines on something whose effect within human earthly evolution is not weak, something that is working powerfully as the deepest meaning of human evolution. The light illumines what we may call the birth of Christianity, the Christmas of Christianity. Along with the Easter meaning of anthroposophical spiritual science may this its Christmas meaning be understood. May many, many souls look forward in this spirit to the profound experience of the Christmas Holy Nights. They will then be able to feel that already a call is sounding through the world to contemplate the appearance of Jesus, who awaited here on earth that moment when He was to meet death, in order in His spirit-life after death to give a new meaning to mankind and to earth evolution.

My dear friends, let us feel something of this Christmas mood that is to enter our souls from spiritual science! I would like at this moment to begin Christmas solemnly, by expressing the wish—as my soul's innermost holy Christmas greeting—that you may experience the mood of consecration that wills to receive the new Christ-revelation. I assume that you too are beginning Christmas with that earnestness of which I endeavored to speak today, an earnestness appropriate to the present condition of the world. In this spirit, my dear friends, I wish you with all my heart a holy, solemn Christmas!

III

When I made some suggestions last Sunday for a renewal of our Christmas thinking, I spoke of the real, inner human being who comes from the spiritual world and unites with the body that is given to him from the stream of heredity. I described how this human being, when he enters the life he is to experience between birth and death, enters it with a certain sense of equality. I said that someone who observes a child with understanding will notice how he does not yet know of the distinctions that exist in the human social structure, due to all the relationships into which men's karma leads them. I said that if we observe clearly and without prejudice the forces residing in certain capacities and talents, even in genius, we shall be compelled to ascribe these in large measure to the impulses which affect mankind through the hereditary stream; that when such impulses appear clearly in the natural course of that stream, we must call them luciferic. Moreover, in our present epoch these impulses will only be fitted into the social structure properly if we recognize them as luciferic, if we are educated to strip off the luciferic element and, in a certain sense, to offer upon the altar of Christ what nature has bestowed upon us— in order to transform it.

There are two opposite points of view: one is concerned with the differences occurring in mankind through heredity and conditions of birth; the other with the fact that the real kernel of a man's being holds within it at the beginning of his earthly life the essential impulse for equality. This shows that the human being is only observed correctly when he is

33

observed through the course of his whole life, when his development in time is really taken into account. We have pointed out in another connection that the developmental motif changes in the course of life. You will also find reference to this in an article I wrote called "The Ahrimanic and the Luciferic in Human Life," where it is shown that the luciferic influence plays a certain role in the first half of life, the ahrimanic in the second half; that both these impulses are active throughout life, but in different ways.

Along with the idea of equality, other ideas have recently been forced into prominence in a tumultuous fashion, in a certain sense precipitating what should have been a tranquil development in the future. They have been set beside the idea of equality, but they should really be worked out slowly in human evolution if they are to contribute to the well-being of humanity and not to disaster. They can only be rightly understood and their significance for life rightly estimated if they are given their proper place in the sequence of a man's life.

Side by side with the idea of equality, the idea of freedom resounds through the modern world. I spoke to you about the idea of freedom some time ago in connection with the new edition of my *Philosophy of Spiritual Activity*. We are therefore able to appreciate the full importance and range of this impulse in relation to the innermost kernel of man's being. Perhaps some of you know that it has frequently been necessary, from questions here and there, to point to the entirely unique character of the conception of freedom as it is delineated in my *Philosophy of Spiritual Activity*. There is a certain fact that I have always found necessary to emphasize in this connection, namely, that the various modern philosophical conceptions of freedom have made the mistake (if you want to call it a mistake) of putting the question thus: Is the human being free or not free? Can we ascribe free will to man? or may we only say that he stands within a kind of absolute natural necessity, and out of this necessity accomplishes his deeds and the resolves of his will? This way of putting the question is incorrect. There is no "either-or." One cannot say, man is either free or unfree. One has to say, man is in the process of development from unfreedom to freedom. And the way the impulse for freedom is conceived in my *Philosophy of Spiritual Activity*, shows you that man is becoming ever freer, that he is extricating himself from necessity, that more and more impulses are growing in him that make it possible for him to be a free being within the rest of the world order.

Thus the impulse for equality has its greater intensity at birth—even though not in consciousness, since the latter is not yet developed—and it then decreases. That is to say, the impulse for equality has a descending development. We may make a diagram thus:

At birth we find the height of the impulse for equality, and it moves in a descending curve. With the impulse for freedom the reverse is true. Freedom moves in an ascending

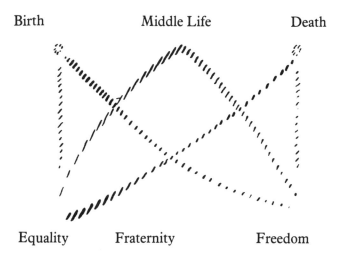

Birth	Middle Life	Death

| Equality | Fraternity | Freedom |

curve and has its culmination at death. By that I do not mean to say that man reaches the summit of a freely-acting being when he passes through the gate of death; but relatively, with regard to human life, a man develops the impulse for freedom increasingly up to the moment of death, and he has achieved relatively the greatest possibility of becoming free at the moment he enters the spiritual world through the gate of death. That is to say: while at birth he brings with him out of the spiritual world the sense of equality which then declines during the course of physical life, it is just during his physical lifetime that he develops the impulse toward freedom, and he then enters the spiritual world through the gate of death with the largest measure of this impulse for freedom that he could attain in the course of his physical life.

You see again how one-sidedly the human being is often observed. One fails to take into account the time element in his being. He is spoken of in general terms, *in abstracto*, because people are not inclined today to consider realities. But man is not a static being; he is an evolving being. The more he develops and the more he makes it possible to develop, so much the more does he fulfill his true task here in the course of physical life. People who are inflexible, who are disinclined to undergo development, accomplish little of their real earthly mission. What you were yesterday you no longer are today, and what you are today you will no longer be tomorrow. These are indeed slight shades of differences; but happy is he in whom they exist at all—for standing still is ahrimanic! There should be shades of difference. No day should pass in a man's life without his receiving at least one thought that alters his nature a little, that enables him to develop instead of merely to exist. Thus we recognize man's true nature—not when we insist in an absolute sense that mankind has the right to freedom and equality in this world —but only when we know that the impulse for equality reaches its culmination at the beginning of life, and the impulse toward freedom at the end. We unravel the complexity of human development in the course of life here on earth only when we take such things into consideration. One cannot simply look abstractly at the whole man and say: he has the right to find freedom, equality, and so forth, within the social structure. These things must be brought to people's attention again through spiritual science, for they have been ignored by the recent developments that move toward abstract ideas and materialism.

The third impulse, *fraternity*, has its culmination, in a certain sense, in the middle of life. Its curve rises and then falls. (See diagram.) In the middle of life, when the human being is in his least rigid condition—that is, when he is vacillating in the relation of soul to body—then it is that he has the strongest tendency to develop brotherliness. He does not always do so, but at this time he has the predisposition to do so. The strongest prerequisites for the development of fraternity exist in middle life.

Thus these three impulses are distributed over an entire lifetime. In the times we are approaching it will be necessary for our understanding of other men, and also—as a matter of course—for our so-called self-knowledge, that we take such matters into account. We cannot arrive at correct ideas about community life unless we know how these impulses are distributed in the course of life. In a certain sense we will be unable to live our lives usefully unless we are willing to gain this knowledge; for we will not know exactly what relation a young man bears to an old man, or an older person to one in middle life, unless we keep in mind the special configuration of these inner impulses.

But now let us connect all this with lectures[5] I gave here earlier about the whole human race gradually becoming younger. Perhaps you recall that I explained how the particular dependence of soul development upon the physical organism that a human being has today only during his very earliest years was experienced in ancient times up to old age. (We are speaking now only of post-Atlantean epochs.) I said that in the ancient Indian cultural epoch man was dependent upon his so-called physical development into his fifties, in the way that he is now dependent only in the earliest years. Now in the first years of life man is dependent upon his physical development. We know the kind of break the change of teeth causes, then puberty, and so on. In these early years we see a distinct parallel in the development of soul and of body; then this ceases, vanishes. I pointed out that in older cultural epochs of our post-Atlantean period that was not the case. The possibility of receiving wisdom from nature simply through being a human being—lofty wisdom which was venerated among the ancient Indians, and could still be venerated among the ancient Persians— that possibility existed because the conditions were not the same as they are now. Now a man becomes a finished product in his twenties; he is then no longer dependent upon his physical organism. Starting from his twenties, it gives him nothing more. This was not the case in ancient times. In ancient times the physical organism itself gave wisdom to man's soul into his fifties. It was possible for him in the second half of life, even without special occult training, to extract the forces from his physical organism in an elemental way, and thus attain a certain wisdom and a certain development of will. I pointed to the significance of this for the ancient Indian and Persian epochs, even for the Egypto-Chaldean epoch, when it was possible to say to a boy or girl, or young man or young woman: "When you are old you may expect that something will come into your life, will be bestowed upon you simply by your having become old, because one continues to develop up to the time of death." Age was looked up to with reverence, because a man said to himself: With old age something will enter my life that I cannot know or cannot will while I am still young. That gave a certain structure to the entire social life which only ceased when during the Greco-Latin epoch this point of time fell back into the middle years of human life. In the ancient Indian civilization man was capable of development up to his fifties. Then during the ancient Persian epoch mankind grew younger: that is, the age of the human race, the capacity for development, fell back to the end of a man's forties. During the Egypto-Chaldean epoch it came between the thirty-fifth and the forty-second year. During the Greco-Latin epoch he was only capable of development up to a point of time between the twenty-eighth and the thirty-fifth year. When the Mystery of Golgotha occurred, he had this capability up to the thirty-third year. This is the wonderful fact we discover in the history of mankind's evolution: that the age of Christ Jesus when he passed through death on Golgotha coincides with the age to which humanity had fallen back at that time.

We pointed out that humanity is still becoming younger and younger; that is, the age at which it is no longer capable of development continues to decrease. This is significant, for example, when today a man enters public life at the particular age at which humanity now stands—twenty-seven years—without having received anything beside what he took in from the outside up to his twenty-seventh year. I mentioned that in this sense Lloyd-George[6] is the representative man of our time. He entered public life at twenty-seven years. This had far-reaching consequences, which you can of course discover by reading his biography. These facts enable one to understand world conditions from within.

Now what strikes you as the most important fact when you connect what we have just been indicating—the increasing youthfulness of the human race—with the thoughts we have brought before our souls in these last days in relation to Christmas? The state of our development since the Mystery of Golgotha is this, that starting from our thirtieth year we can really gain nothing from our own organism, from what is bestowed upon us by nature. If the Mystery of Golgotha had not taken place, we would be going about here on earth after our 30th year saying to ourselves: Actually we live in the true sense only up to our thirty-second or thirty-third year at most. Up to that time our organism makes it possible for us to live; then we might just as well die. For from the course of nature, from the elemental occurrences of nature, we can gain nothing more for our soul development through the impulses of our organism. If the Mystery of Golgotha had not taken place, the earth would be filled with human beings lamenting thus: Of what use to me is life after my thirty-third year? Up to that time my organism can give me something. After that I might just as well be dead. I really go about here on earth like a living corpse. If the Mystery of Golgotha had not taken place, many people would feel that they are going about on earth like living corpses. But the Mystery of Golgotha, dear friends, has still to be made fruitful. We should not merely receive the Impulse of Golgotha unconsciously, as people now do: we should receive it consciously, in such a manner that through it we may remain youthful up to old age. And it can indeed keep us healthy and youthful if we receive it consciously in the right way. We shall then be conscious of its enlivening effect upon our life. This is important!

Thus you see that the Mystery of Golgotha can be regarded as something intensely alive during the course of our earthly life. I said earlier that people are most predisposed to brotherliness in the middle of life—around the thirty-third year, but they do not always develop it. You have the reason for this in what I have just said. Those who fail to develop brotherliness, who lack something of brotherliness, simply are too little permeated by the Christ. Since the human being begins to die, in a certain sense, in middle age from the forces of nature, he cannot properly develop the impulse, the instinct, of brotherliness—and still less the impulse toward freedom, which is taken up so little today—unless he brings to life within himself thoughts that come directly from the Christ Impulse. When we turn to the Christ Impulse, it enkindles brotherliness in us directly. To the degree to which a man feels the necessity for brotherliness, he is permeated by Christ.

One is also unable alone to develop the impulse for freedom to full strength during the remainder of one's earthly life. (In future periods of evolution this will be different.) Something entered our earth evolution as human being and flowed forth at the death of Christ Jesus to unite Itself with the earthly evolution of humanity. Therefore Christ is the One who also leads present-day mankind to freedom. We become free in Christ when we are able to grasp the fact that the Christ could really not have become older, could not have lived longer, in a physical body than up to the age of thirty-three years. Suppose hypothetically that He had lived longer: then He would have lived on in a physical body into the years when according to our present earth evolution this body is destined for death. The Christ would have taken up the forces of death. Had he lived to be forty years old, He would have experienced the forces of death in His body. These He would not have wished to experience. He could only have wished to experience those forces that are still the freshening forces for a human being. He was active up to His thirty-third year, to the middle of life; as the Christ He enkindled brotherliness. Then He caused the spirit to flow into human evolution: He gave over to the Holy Spirit what was henceforth to be within the power of man. Through this Holy Spirit, this health-giving Spirit, a human being develops to freedom toward the end of his life. Thus is the Christ Impulse integrated into the concrete life of humanity.

This permeation of man's inner being by the Christ

Principle must be incorporated into human knowledge as a new Christmas thought. Mankind must know that we bring equality with us out of the spiritual world. It comes, one might say, from God the Father, and is given to us to bring to earth. Then brotherliness reaches its proper culmination only through the help of the Son. And through the Christ united with the Spirit we can develop the impulse for freedom as we draw near to death.

This activity of the Christ Impulse in the concrete shaping of humanity is something that from now on must be accepted consciously by human souls. This alone will be really health-giving when people's demands for refashioning the social structure become more and more urgent and passionate. In this social structure there live children, youths, middle-aged and old people; and a social structure that embraces them all can only be achieved when it is realized that human beings are not simply abstract Man. The five-year-old child is Man, the twenty-year-old youth, the twenty-year-old young woman, the forty-year-old man—all are Man. But this chaotic mixture does not lead to such knowledge of man as is necessary to fulfill the demands of the future, or even of the present. Such confusion gives rise at most to the thought: A man is Man, therefore at about the age of twenty he must be elected to Parliament. These things are destructive to the true social organism. They rest upon people's unwillingness at the present time to undertake an actual observation of human beings, which would result in a consciousness of humanity in the concrete, human beings as they really are. When they are looked at concretely, the abstraction Man-Man-Man has no reality whatsoever. There can only be the fact of a specific human being of a specific age with specific impulses. Knowledge of Man must be acquired, but it can only be acquired by studying the development of the essential living kernel of the human being as he progresses from birth to death. That must come, my dear friends. And probably people will not be inclined to receive such things into their consciousness until they are again able to take a retrospective view of the evolution of mankind.

Yesterday I drew your attention to something that entered human evolution with Christianity. Christianity was born out of the Jewish soul, the Greek spirit, and the Roman body. These were the sheaths, so to speak, of Christianity. But within Christianity is the living Ego, and this can be separately observed when we look back to the birth of Christianity. For the external historian this birth of Christianity has become very chaotic. What is usually written today about the early centuries of Christianity, whether from a Roman Catholic or a Protestant point of view, is very confused wisdom. The essence of much that existed in those first Christian centuries is either entirely forgotten by present theologians or else it has become, may I say, an abomination for them. Just read and observe the strange convulsions of intellectualism—they almost become a kind of intellectual epilepsy—when people have to describe what lived in the first centuries of Christianity as the Gnosis.[7] It is considered a sort of devil, this Gnosis, something so demonic that it should absolutely not be admitted into human life. And when such a theologian or other official representative of this or that denomination can accuse anthroposophy of having something in common with gnosticism, he believes he has made the worst possible charge.

Underlying all this is the fact that in the earliest centuries of Christianity gnosticism did indeed penetrate the spiritual life of European humanity—so far as this was of importance for the civilization of that time—and, moreover, much more significantly than is now supposed. There exists on the one hand, not the slightest idea of what this Gnosis actually was; on the other hand, I might say, there is a mysterious fear of it. To most of the present-day official representatives of any religious denomination the Gnosis is something horrible. But it can of course be looked at without sympathy or antipathy, purely objectively. Then it would best be studied from a spiritual scientific standpoint, for external history has little to offer. Western ecclesiastical development took care that all external remains of the Gnosis were properly eradicated, root and branch. There is very little left, as you know—only the *Pistis Sophia* and the like—and that gives only a vague idea of it. Otherwise the only passages from the Gnosis that are known are those refuted by the Church Fathers. That means really that the Gnosis is only known from the writings of opponents, while anything that might have given some idea of it from an external, historical point of view has been thoroughly rooted out.

An intellectual study of the development of Western theology would make people more critical on this point as well—but such study is rare. It would show them, for instance, that Christian dogma must surely have its foundation in something quite different from caprice or the like. Actually, it is all rooted in the Gnosis. But its living force has been stripped away and abstract thoughts, concepts, the mere hulls are left, so that one no longer recognizes in the doctrines their living origin. Nevertheless, it is really the Gnosis. If you study the Gnosis as far as it can be studied with spiritual scientific methods, you will find a certain light is thrown upon the few things that have been left to history by the opponents of gnosticism. And you will probably realize that this Gnosis points to the very widespread and concrete atavistic-clairvoyant world conception of ancient times. There were considerable remnants of this in the first post-Atlantean epoch, less in the second. In the third epoch the final remnants were worked upon and appeared as gnosticism in a remarkable system of concepts, concepts that are extraordinarily figurative. Anyone who studies gnosticism from this standpoint, who is able to go back, even just

44

historically, to the meager remnants—they are brought to light more abundantly in the pagan Gnosis than in Christian literature—will find that, as a matter of fact, this Gnosis contained wonderful treasures of wisdom relating to a world with which people of our present age refuse to have any connection. So it is not at all surprising that even well-intentioned people can make little of the ancient Gnosis.

Well-intentioned people? I mean, for instance, people like Professor Jeremias of Leipzig, who would indeed be willing to study these things. But he can form no mental picture of what these ancient concepts refer to—when, for example, mention is made of a spiritual being Jaldabaoth, who is supposed with a sort of arrogance to have declared himself ruler of the world, then to have been reprimanded by his mother, and so on. Even from what has been historically preserved, such mighty images radiate to us as the following: Jaldabaoth said, "I am God the Father; there is no one above me." And his mother answered, "Do not lie! Above thee is the Father of all, the first Man, and the Son of Man." Then—it is further related—Jaldabaoth called his six co-workers and they said, "Let us make man in our image." Such imaginations, quite self-explanatory, were numerous and extensive in what existed as the Gnosis. In the Old Testament we find only remnants of this pictorial wisdom preserved by Jewish tradition. It lived especially in the Orient, whence its rays reached the West; and only in the third or fourth century did these begin to fade in the West. But then there were still some after-effects among the Waldenses and Cathars[8] that finally died out.

People of our time can hardly imagine the condition of the souls living in civilized Europe during the first Christian centuries, in whom there lived not merely mental pictures like those of present-day Roman Catholics, but in a supreme degree vivid, unmistakable echoes of this mighty world-picture of the Gnosis. What we see when we look back at those souls is vastly different from what we find in books that have been written about these centuries by ecclesiastical and secular theologians and other scholars. In the books there is nothing of all that lived in those great and powerful imaginative pictures describing a world of which, as I have said, people of our time have no conception. That is why a man possessing present-day scholarship can do nothing with such concepts—for instance, with Jaldabaoth, his mother, the six co-workers, and so on. He does not know what to do with them. They are words, word-husks; what they refer to, he does not know. Still less does he know how the people of that earlier age ever came to form such concepts. A modern person can only say, "Well, of course, the ancient Orientals had lively imaginations; they developed all that fantasy." We ourselves must marvel that such a person has not the slightest idea how little imagination a primitive human being has, what a minor role it plays, for instance, among peasants. In this respect the mythologists have done wonders! They have invented the stories of simple people transforming the drifting clouds, the wind driving the clouds, and so on, into all sorts of beings. They have no idea how the earlier humanity to whom they attribute all this were really constituted in their souls, that they were as far removed as could possibly be from such poetic fashioning. The fantasy really exists in the circles of the mythologists, the scholars who think out such things. That is the real fantasy!

What people suppose to have been the origin of mythology is pure error. They do not know today to what its words and concepts refer. Certain, may I say, clear hints concerning their interpretation are therefore no longer given any serious attention. Plato pointed very precisely to the fact that a human being living here in a physical body has remembrance of something experienced in the spiritual world before this physical life. But present-day philosophers can make nothing of this Platonic memory-knowledge; for them it is something that Plato too had imagined. In reality, Plato still knew with certainty that the Greek soul was predisposed to unfold in itself what it had experienced in the spiritual world before birth, though it still possessed only the last residue of this ability. Anyone who between birth and death perceives only by means of his physical body and who works over his perceptions with a present-day intellect, cannot grant any rational meaning to observations that have not even been made in a physical body but were made between death and a new birth. Before birth human beings were in a world in which they could speak of Jaldabaoth who rose up in pride, whose mother admonished him, who summoned the six co-workers. That is a reality for the human being between death and a new birth, just as plants, animals, minerals, and other human beings are realities for him here in this world, about which he speaks when he is confined in a physical body. The Gnosis contained what was brought into this physical world at birth; and it was possible to a certain extent up to the Egypto-Chaldean epoch, that is, up to the eighth century before the Christian era, for human beings to bring very much with them from the time they had spent between death and a new birth. What was brought in those epochs from the spiritual world and clothed in concepts, in ideas, is the Gnosis. It continued to exist in the Greco-Latin epoch, but it was no longer directly perceived; it was a heritage existing now as ideas. Its origin was known only to select spirits such as Plato, in a lesser degree to Aristotle also. Socrates knew of it too, and indeed paid for this knowledge with his death.

Now what were the conditions in this Greco-Latin age in the fourth post-Atlantean epoch? Only meager recollections of time before birth could now be brought over into life, but something was brought over, and in this Greek period it was still distinct. People today are inordinately proud of their power of thinking, but actually they can grasp very little with it. The thinking power that the Greeks developed was of a different nature. When the Greeks entered earthly life through birth, the images of their experiences before birth were lost; but the thinking force that they had used before birth to give an intelligent meaning to the images still remained. Greek thinking differed completely from our so-called normal thinking, for the Greek thinking was the result of pondering over imaginations that had been experienced before birth. Of the imaginations themselves little was recalled; the essential thing that remained was the discernment that had helped a person before birth to find his way in the world about which imaginations had been formed. The waning of this thinking power was the important factor in the development of the fourth post-Atlantean period, which continued, as you know, into the fifteenth century of the Christian era.

Now in this fifth epoch the power to think must again be developed, out of our earthly culture. Slowly, haltingly, we must develop it out of the scientific world view. Today we are at the beginning of it. During the fourth post-Atlantean period, that is, from 747 B.C. to 1413 A.D.—the Event of Golgotha lies between—there was a continual decrease of thinking power. Only in the fifteenth century did it begin slowly to rise again; by the third millennium it will once more have reached a considerable height. Of our present-day power of thought mankind need not be especially proud; it has declined. The thinking power, still highly developed, that was the heritage of the Greeks shaped the thoughts with which the gnostic pictures were set in order and mastered. Although the pictures were no longer as clear as they had been for the Egyptians or the Babylonians, for example, the thinking power was still there. But it gradually faded. That is the extraordinary way things worked together in the earliest Christian centuries.

The Mystery of Golgotha breaks upon the world. Christianity is born. The waning thinking power, still very active in the Orient but also reaching over into Greece, tried to understand this event. The Romans had little understanding of it. This thinking power tried to understand the Event of Golgotha from the standpoint of the thinking used before birth, the thinking of the spiritual world. And now something significant occurred: this gnostic thinking came face to face with the Mystery of Golgotha. Now let us consider the gnostic teachings about the Mystery of Golgotha, which are such an abomination to present-day, especially Christian, theologians. Much is to be found in them from the ancient atavistic teachings, or from teachings that are permeated by the ancient thought-force; and many significant and impressive things are said in them about the Christ that today are termed heretical, shockingly heretical. Gradually this power of gnostic thought declined. We still see it in Manes[9] in the third century, and we still see it as it passes over to the Cathars—downright heretics from the Catholic point of view: a great, forceful, grandiose interpretation of the Mystery of Golgotha. This ebbed away, strangely enough, in the early centuries, and people were little inclined to apply any effort toward an understanding of the Mystery of Golgotha. These two things, you see, were engaged in a struggle: the gnostic teaching, wishing to comprehend the Mystery of Golgotha through powerful spiritual thinking; and the other teaching, that reckoned with what was to come, when thought would no longer have power, when it would lack the penetration needed to understand the Mystery of Golgotha, when it would be abstract and unfruitful. The Mystery of Golgotha, a cosmic mystery, was reduced to hardly more than a few sentences at the beginning of the *Gospel of St. John*, telling of the Logos, of His entrance into the world and His destiny in the world, using as few concepts as possible; for what had to be taken into account was the decreasing thinking power.

Thus the gnostic interpretation of Christianity gradually died out, and a different conception of it arose, using as few concepts as possible. But of course the one passed over into the other: concepts like the dogma of the Trinity were taken over from gnostic ideas and reduced to abstractions, mere husks of concepts. The really vital fact is this, that an inspired gnostic interpretation of the Mystery of Golgotha was engaged in a struggle with the other explanation, which worked with as few concepts as possible, estimating what humanity would be like by the fifteenth century with the ancient, hereditary, acute thinking power declining more and more. It was also reckoning that this would eventually have to be acquired again, in elementary fashion, through the scientific observation of nature. You can study it step by step. You can even perceive it as an inner soul-struggle if you observe St. Augustine,[10] who in his youth became acquainted with gnostic Manichaeism, but could not digest that and so turned away to so-called "simplicity," forming primitive concepts. These became more and more primitive. Even so, in Augustine there appeared the first dawning light of what had again to be acquired: knowledge starting from man, from the concrete human being. In ancient gnostic times one had tried to reach the human being by starting from the world. Now, henceforth, the start must be made from man: knowledge of the world must be acquired from knowledge of the human being. This must be the direction we take in the future. I explained this here some time ago and tried to point to the first dawning light in humanity. One finds it, for instance, in the *Confessions of St. Augustine* —but it was still thoroughly chaotic. The essential fact is that humanity became more and more incapable of taking in what streamed to it from the spiritual world, what had existed among the ancients as imaginative wisdom and then was active in the Gnosis, what had evoked the power of acute thinking that still existed among the Greeks. Thus the

Greek wisdom, even though reduced to abstract concepts, still provided the ideas that allowed some understanding of the spiritual world. This then ceased; nothing of the spiritual world could any longer be understood through those dying ideas.

A man of the present day can easily feel that the Greek ideas are in fact applicable to something entirely different from that to which they were applied. This is a peculiarity of Hellenism. The Greeks still had the ideas but no longer the imaginations. Especially in Aristotle this is very striking. It is very singular. You know there are whole libraries about Aristotle, and everything concerning him is interpreted differently. People even dispute whether he accepted reincarnation or pre-existence. This has all come about because his words can be interpreted in various ways. It is because he worked with a system of concepts applicable to a supersensible world but he no longer had any perception of that world. Plato had much more understanding of it; therefore his system of concepts could be worked out better in that sense. Aristotle was already involved in abstract concepts and could no longer see that to which his thought-forms referred. It is a peculiar fact that in the early centuries there was a struggle between a conception of the Mystery of Golgotha that illuminated it with the light of the supersensible world, and the fanaticism that then developed to refute this. Not everyone saw through these things, but some did. Those who did see through them did not face them honestly. A primitive interpretation of the Mystery of Golgotha, an interpretation that was rabid about using only a few concepts, led to fanaticism.

Thus we see that supersensible thinking was eliminated more and more from the Christian world conception, from every world conception. It faded away and ceased. We can follow from century to century how the Mystery of Golgotha appeared to people as something tremendously significant

51

that had entered earth evolution, and yet how the possibility of their comprehending it with any system of concepts vanished—or of comprehending the world cosmically at all. Look at that work from the ninth century, *De Divisione Naturae* by Scotus Erigena.[11] It still contains pictures of a world evolution, even though the pictures are abstract. Scotus Erigena indicates very beautifully four stages of a world evolution, but throughout with inadequate concepts. We can see that he is unable to spread out his net of concepts and make intelligible, plausible, what he wishes to gather together. Everywhere, one might say, the threads of his concepts break. It is very interesting that this becomes more noticeable from century to century, so that finally the lowest point in the spinning of concept-threads was reached in the fifteenth century. Then an ascent began again, but it did not get beyond the most elementary stage. It is interesting that on the one hand people cherished the Mystery of Golgotha and turned to it with their hearts, but declared that they could not understand it. Gradually there was a general feeling that it could not be understood. On the other hand the study of nature began at the very time when concepts vanished. Observation of nature entered the life of that time, but there were no concepts for actually grasping the phenomena that were being observed.

It is characteristic of this period, at the turn of the fourth to the fifth post-Atlantean epoch, halfway through the Middle Ages, that there were insufficient concepts both for the budding observation of nature and for the revelations of saving truths. Think how it was with Scholasticism in this respect: it had religious revelations, but no concepts out of the culture of the time that would enable it to work over these religious revelations. It had to employ Aristotelianism; this had to be revived. The Scholastics went back to Hellenism, to Aristotle, to find concepts with which to penetrate the religious revelations; and they elaborated these with the

Greek intellect because the culture of their own time had no intellect of its own—if I may use such a paradox. So the very people who worked the most honestly, the Scholastics, did not use the intellect of their time, because there was none, none that belonged to their culture. It was characteristic of the period from the tenth to the fifteenth century that the most honest of the Scholastics made use of the ancient Aristotelian concepts to explain natural phenomena; they also employed them to formulate religious revelations. Only thereafter did there rise again, as from hoary depths of spirit, an independent mode of thinking—not very far developed, even to this day—the thinking of Copernicus and Galileo. This must be further developed in order to rise once more to supersensible regions.

Thus we are able to look into the soul, into the ego, so to speak, of Christianity, which had merely clothed itself with the Jewish soul, the Greek spirit, and the Roman body. This ego of Christianity had to take into account the dying-out of supersensible understanding, and therefore had to permit the comprehensive gnostic wisdom to shrink, as it were—one may even say, to shrink to the few words at the beginning of the *Gospel of John*. For the evolution of Christianity consists essentially of the victory of the words of St. John's Gospel over the content of the Gnosis. Then, of course, everything passed over into fanaticism, and gnosticism was exterminated, root and branch.

All these things are linked to the birth of Christianity. We must take them into consideration if we want to receive a real impulse for the consciousness of humanity that must be developed anew, and an impulse for the new Christmas thought. We must come again to a kind of knowledge that relates to the supersensible. To that end we must understand the supersensible force working into the being of man, so that we may be able to extend it to the cosmos. We must acquire anthroposophy, knowledge of the human being, which will be able to engender cosmic feeling again. That is the way. In ancient times man could survey the world, because he entered his body at birth with memories of the time before birth. This world, which is a likeness of the spiritual world, was an answer to questions he brought with him into this life. Now the human being confronts this world bringing nothing with him, and he must work with primitive concepts like those, for instance, of contemporary science. But he must work his way up again; he must now start from the human being and rise to the cosmos. Knowledge of the cosmos must be born in the human being. This too belongs to a conception of Christmas that must be developed in the present epoch, in order that it may be fruitful in the future.

IV

We tried two days ago to point to the impulses from which Christianity developed. We could see how the real Ego of Christianity, the essence of Christianity, embodied itself, as it were (one cannot say that, of course, except by way of comparison)—embodied itself in three elements: the ancient Hebrew soul, the Greek spirit, and the Roman body. In order to be able to apply these thoughts to the immediate present, today we will carry them a little further, and try to gain a few more glimpses of this inner being of Christianity.

If we wish to trace the development of Christianity, we must show to what extent it has evolved from the Mysteries of pre-Christian times. (You will have found this already in my book, *Christianity as Mystical Fact*.) Today it is not easy to speak of the general nature of the Mysteries, because in the course of human evolution, happening as it did in conformity to cosmic law, the epoch arrived—in a sense we are still in it—in which the Mysteries declined. They could no longer play the role they had played at the time when Christianity was evolving out of them—as also out of other things. There is good reason for the decadence of the Mysteries in our time; we will be able to go into this in our discussion today and the following days. We will also be able to see in what way the Mysteries are to be established anew.

I shall speak first, then, of pre-Christian times, let us say to begin with, of pre-Christian Greek and pre-Christian Egypto-Chaldean epochs. What impelled people to seek out the Mysteries in those ancient times was this: their world conception forced them to believe that the world they saw spread out around them was not in itself the true world, but that they must find the means of penetrating to the true world. They had a strong sense for a certain fact when they faced any riddles of knowledge: they knew that however one tries to discover the true nature of the world by external means, it is impossible to do so. For one to realize the full importance of this knowledge that people possessed in ancient times, one must remember that we are speaking of an era in which most human beings still had a completely objective view of elementary spiritual facts. Conditions then were entirely different from those of today: people in those days not only received the impressions of their outer senses; they also still perceived spiritual realities within the phenomena of nature. They perceived activities that were by no means limited to what we today call processes of nature. Nevertheless, although they spoke generally of the manifestation of elemental spirits in nature, they had a deep knowledge that these observations of the external world, however clairvoyant, did not lead to the true being of the world, that this true being of the world must be sought by special paths. These special paths were beautifully summed up in the Greek world conception in the words, "Know thou thyself!"

If we look for the real meaning of the words "Know thou thyself!", we will find something like the following: their power comes from the insight that to whatever extent we may survey the external world or penetrate into it, we will not only fail to find the being of this outer world but we will also fail to find the being of man. Expressing it simply, in the sense of our present-day world view, we could say: those ancient people believed that a conception of nature could give no explanation of the being of man. On the contrary, they were convinced that the being of man is connected with the whole of nature spread out in the world; therefore, if a man succeeded in penetrating into his own being, he would then be able through knowledge of his own being to gain an understanding of the being of the world as well. Therefore, "Know thou thyself in order to know the world!": that was the impulse, one might say; and that impulse formed the basis of—well, let us say, of the Egypto-Chaldean initiation. All initiation proceeds by stages; we have become accustomed to call them degrees. Now, we may characterize the first stage, the first degree, of the Egypto-Chaldean initiation in this way: the neophyte must first pass through the "gate of man." That means, the human being himself was to be the gate of knowledge. First the human being must be understood, because if we learn to know the being of man through man himself, then we can penetrate into the being of the world indirectly through man. Hence, "Know thou thyself!" is synonymous with entrance into the being of the world through the "gate of man."

It is not my intention to speak in detail today about the stages of Egypto-Chaldean initiation; I would like to point out what is essential for the understanding of Christianity. Therefore, do not regard what I shall say as an exhaustive presentation. I wish simply to mention single characteristics of those stages, which could and did have a particular preparatory influence upon the development of the being of Christianity.

What the neophyte at the "gate of man" was to learn to know, therefore, was the being of man himself. That was something he could not find in what the outer world revealed to him, however far and carefully he sought. In the Mysteries it was known that some of the secrets of existence had remained in human nature and could be discovered by human means, secrets that could not be found by searching the outer world. Those ancient people were convinced of this. If one directs his attention to the outer world, he finds, of course, first of all the earthly substances and forces surrounding him. But these earthly substances and forces, so far as man understands them, are only a kind of veil. Whatever natural science may now have to say about external nature as it presents itself, is such that it throws no light whatever upon it. In earlier times the human being could look up from external nature that he saw around him on earth to the world of the stars; and in those ancient times he did that much more intensively than he does today. There he saw many things, and he well knew in those times that man is related to them just as he is related to the plant, animal, and mineral kingdoms on earth. This is a knowledge that has disappeared from the outer world today. Ancient man knew that just as he is born out of the kingdoms of nature on earth, something in him is also born out of the extra-tellurian, extra-earthly cosmos. Indeed, it was this connection of the human being to the cosmos beyond the earth that became known to him when he passed through the "gate of man." He bore within him, one might say, remnants of the relationship that he had discarded in his transition from Moon-nature to Earth-nature. He bore within him the remnants of his relationship to the cosmos beyond the earth. So he was led to the "gate of man," where he was to become acquainted with man himself. He came to know in himself what externally he could only gaze at, especially in the world of the stars.

In himself he learned that as a true human being not only is he organized in an earthly body gathered from the kingdoms of earthly nature, but also something coming from beyond the earth, coming from the whole world of the stars, has flowed into his entire human entity. A man discovered the nature of the starry sky, one might say, through knowledge of himself. He came to know how he had descended step by step, descended from heaven to heaven, so to say, before he reached the earth and incarnated in an earthly body. And through the "gate of man" he was to ascend these steps again—eight of them were usually specified. During his initiation he was to set out on the return, through the stages by which he had descended to his birth in a physical body. Such insight could not be gained without man's whole nature being profoundly affected. (I am speaking now always of the pre-Christian Mystery knowledge.) The man of today does not even like to form an idea of the preparation that the neophyte had to go through in those times, because these ideas irritate him. (I am choosing my words so as to express the facts as exactly as possible.) A modern person would like to undergo initiation, if possible, as something to be done casually somewhere along his life-path, something to be done incidentally. He would like to inquire—as people say today—into what leads to knowledge; but in any case, he would not like to experience what the people of old seeking initiation had to experience. To be deeply affected in his whole being by the preparation for knowledge, to become a different man—that he would not like. Those ancient people had to decide to become different human beings. The descriptions you very often find of the ancient Mysteries give you only a dim picture; they create the impression that the ancient initiations were conferred upon individuals just as casually as are, let us say, the so-called initiations of modern Freemasonry. But that was not the case. Where ancient initiations are imitated today, we have to do merely with all sorts of counterfeits of what was really lived through in those ancient times—imitations that can be performed now as superficially as the modern person may wish. But the essential preparation for the man of old was this: he had to go through an inner soul-condition that, if characterized by one word, must be called fear. He had to experience to a most intense degree the fear that is always felt by someone who is brought face to face with something wholly unknown to him. In the ancient initiations that was the essential condition: that an individual should have the most intense feeling of facing something that would not be met with anywhere in external life.

Given all the soul-forces the man of today expends upon his external life, this soul-condition would today still never be reached. With the soul-forces he likes to use he can eat and drink, he can conform to the social customs of the various classes of society recognized today, he can carry on a business, play the bureaucrat, even become a professor or a scientist—all that: but with these capacities actually he can know nothing whatever that is real. The condition of soul in which an individual sought enlightenment in those ancient times—remember that I am speaking now steadily about that ancient time—the condition of soul was essentially different.

It could have nothing in common with the soul-forces that are serviceable for external life; it had to be derived from entirely different regions of the human being. These regions are always present in man, but he has a terrible fear of using them in any way. In the neophyte they were brought into activity in a direct and purposeful way. They are that very part of a human being that is avoided by modern man—by the ordinary, secular man of ancient times too —in which modern man does not want to become involved, and concerning which he likes to have illusions or to be indifferent. One must understand the inner significance of what can be described outwardly as the cause of a series of fear-conditions that had to be undergone. Only what lies in the realm of the soul that man fears in his ordinary external life: only this could be used to attain the desired knowledge. This condition of soul was really experienced in those times, and bravely gone through—a condition in which all the individual felt was fear: fear of something unknown. This fear was to lead him to knowledge. Only through this soul-condition was he then brought face to face with what I have just characterized as the descent of the human being through the regions of heaven, that is, of the spiritual world, to which he was led up again through the eight stages. Naturally, these are only imitated today, as they must be because of the customs of our time; but in those days a man was actually brought to this experience.

Especially important for us is what resulted for the individual who was brought to this "gate of man." When he had grasped the full meaning of being placed there, he no longer considered himself the animal-on-two-legs—pardon the expression—that is, a synthesis of the rest of the kingdoms of nature here on earth. He began to feel himself as belonging to the heavens one can see and also to those one cannot see. He began to consider himself a citizen of the whole world, to feel himself really as microcosm, not merely a little earth, but a little world. He felt his connection with the planets and fixed stars, that he had been born out of the universe. He felt that his being did not end with his fingertips, the tips of his ears, the tips of his toes, but that it extended beyond his body taken from the earth, that his being extended through endless spaces and on through these endless spaces into the realms of spirit. That was the result.

Do not try to form too abstract a concept of this result! To say that man is a microcosm, a little world, and then to have nothing but the abstract idea is not worth much; it is only a delusion, a deception. The matter of importance in those ancient Mysteries was the direct experience. The neophyte really experienced at the "gate of man" his relationship to Mercury, Mars, the Sun, Jupiter, the Moon. He really experienced the connection between his own existence and those hieroglyphs standing in cosmic space through which the sun takes its course ("apparently"—as we say today), the pictures of the zodiac. Only this concrete knowledge based on his immediate experience determined what I am now pointing to as result. When these things are changed today into abstract concepts, the result is not the same. When ancient experiences are converted today into such concepts as: this star has this influence, that star has that influence, and so on, they are nothing but abstract ideas. In those ancient times the thing that mattered was the immediate experience, the actual ascent through the various stages by which a man had descended to birth. Only when the neophyte had this *living* consciousness, only when he experienced that he was a microcosm, was he considered ready to ascend to a second stage, a second degree, which at that time was the real stage of self-knowledge. Then he could experience what he himself was.

Thus what I have characterized as Being, as also the Being of the World, was to be found by a person of that time only in himself; if he wished to find his way into the universe, he had to go through the "gate of man." In the second stage, everything that had been learnt in the first as experienced knowledge began to take on motion. It is difficult today to give any idea of this coming-into-motion of one's experiences. In this second stage the neophyte not only knew that he belongs to the macrocosm, but he was woven into the whole movement of the macrocosm. He went with the sun through the zodiac, as it were, and from this journey through the whole zodiac he came to know the full effect of any outer impression upon man himself. When you confront the external world with only the ordinary means of knowledge, you perceive merely the beginning of a very detailed process. You see a color; you form an image of it; perhaps you retain this image in your memory—and it goes no further. These are three steps. If we were to consider this complete, it would be precisely as if we considered the course of the day, which is twelve hours of sunlight, as consisting only of three hours. For the outer impressions a person receives and follows up, at most, as far as the memory-image, continue within him by a further process beyond the memory-image through nine more steps. The man then becomes a mobile being, inwardly permeated, as it were, by a living, turning wheel, just as the sun describes its heavenly circle ("apparently," according to our present-day concepts). In this way the neophyte came to know himself, and thereby to know also the mysteries of the great world. As he learned in the first stage how he stands within the world, so he learned in the second stage how he moves within the world.

Without this knowledge as life-knowledge, no neophyte in ancient times could reach what he then had to experience at the third stage of initiation. We live now in an epoch in which it is natural for people to disavow completely everything three-membered—speaking in the sense of the Mysteries—to erase utterly from human consciousness everything of a three-membered nature. Whether they admit it or not, the people of our time really presuppose that the entire universe is enclosed in space and time. You will find that even very thoughtful people hold this opinion. You need only recall, for example, how the idea of human immortality was conceived in that part of the nineteenth century when materialism, theoretical materialism, had reached its height. Very clever people in the middle and the second half of the nineteenth century were insisting that if men's souls were to separate from them at death, there would finally be no room; the world would be so filled with souls that there would be no space for them. Very clever people said this, because they assumed that after death a man's soul would have to be taken care of in some way that could only be thought of with space concepts. Or take another example: There was—and it is said to exist still—a Theosophical Society in which all sorts of things were taught about the higher members of man's nature. I do not say that the enlightened leaders fell into this error; but a large proportion of the members imagined the astral body as quite spatial—of course, very tenuous, like a cloud, but nevertheless like a spatial cloud, and they indulged in speculation as to the whereabouts of this cloud in space when someone goes to sleep and the cloud goes out of him spatially. It was difficult to suggest to many of these members that such spatial concepts are unsuitable for spiritual ideas.

It is exceedingly difficult for anyone in our time to imagine that at a certain point on the path of knowledge one does not merely enter into a different dimension of space and time from that of everyday consciousness, but one actually goes out of space and time. The truly supersensible does not really begin until one has abandoned not only sense impressions and their time processes, but space and time themselves. One enters into conditions of existence entirely different from those that have to do with space and time. If you would apply this to yourselves, you might find it difficult to answer the question: What must I do in order to leave space and time with my thinking? Yet that was the real achievement resulting from the completion of the first two stages of the Mysteries. If a clear consciousness of the secrets of the third stage had still existed in this age of materialism, nothing so grotesque could have developed as the theory of spiritism. (I speak now of the basic theory, not of external experimentation.) Anyone who tries to find spirits, wanting to bring them into space as rarefied bodies, does not realize that the procedure is utterly devoid of spirit; that is, he is seeking a world that does not contain spirits but contains something else. Had spiritism had any idea that to find spirits it is necessary to go out of space and time, such grotesque concepts could never have arisen as that of the need for spatial arrangements, so that the spirits can announce themselves by external acts within space and time!

Well, briefly, this is what had to be achieved in the first two stages: the ability to get out of space and time. The preparation for it was the striding through the "gate of man," and then through the second stage.

The third stage was designated by an expression which perhaps we can translate into these words: the neophyte passed through the "gate of death." That means, he knew that now he was really outside space—in which human life is spent between birth and death, and outside time—in which this human life takes its course. He knew how to move beyond space and time, in duration. He came to know something that extends into the sense world, as I have often emphasized, but that cannot be comprehended in the sense world through what it brings, because what it brings, what it contains is spiritual. He learnt about death and all that is connected with it. That was the essential content of this third stage. However we may regard the Mystery rites, varying as they did among the different peoples, however they may be represented, their fundamental concern was with death. Everywhere the starting-point for the third stage had to be the possibility of a man experiencing within the life of the body all that normally he can only experience when death takes him out of the body. (I have to use a paradoxical expression for lack of something better.) This was connected with the possibility of considering the human being as he normally exists between birth and death as something different, something apart from the being whom the neophyte had now become in the third stage. The neophyte had now learnt in connection with the phrase "to be outside the body" to conceive of the "outside" not as spatial, but as super-spatial. He had learnt to connect with these words a concept that could be experienced. It was at this point also that the neophyte laid aside his connection to the ordinary secular religion of his people. Most of all, he laid aside at the "gate of death" the idea that he stood here upon earth while his God or his Gods were somewhere outside him. He knew himself at this moment to be one with his God; he no longer differentiated himself from his God, but knew that he was completely united with Him. It was really the experiencing

65

of immortality that this third stage gave to man, in the experience that a man could cast off his mortal part, could separate himself from his mortal part.

But, dear friends, in contemplating the result, let us not forget the entire path, which consisted in the human being coming to know himself. That is the central feature of this pre-Christian initiation, that the human being turned inward in order to find in himself something that he could then take with him into the outer world. This appeared to him then in the right light only after he had separated himself from himself, so that he felt united with the being of the outer world. He turned inward in order to go out of himself. He turned inward to find what he could only find within himself: the being of the world. He could not first have found it outside; now he could really experience it. He went through the "gate of man," the "gate of self-knowledge," and the "gate of death" in order to enter into the world which was, of course, outside him, into the ordinary world of nature—it is also, of course, outside us—but he knew with certainty that he could only find what he sought in it by turning inward.

After, then, he had passed through the extraordinarily difficult third stage, he was at once ready for the fourth. And one may say that simply through having practiced living at the third stage for a certain time, he was prepared for the fourth in a way that would hardly apply to a man of the present day. For the man of today, simply because of the epoch of time, does not become fully mature in the third stage. He does not easily get away from conceptions of space and time except through certain ideas of force—and these too have to be sought by different methods from those of ancient times. (I will speak about this in coming lectures.) By what the neophyte had now carried into the world from out of himself, he was raised to the consciousness of the fourth stage: he became what was expressed, when carried over and translated into later languages, by the word Christo-phorus, or Christ-bearer. That was fundamentally the goal of this Mystery-initiation: to make the human being a Christ-bearer. Naturally, only a few selected individuals became Christ-bearers. Moreover, they could only become such by first seeking in themselves what was not to be found in the outer world, by then taking back into the outer world what they had found within, and then by uniting themselves with their God. This is the way they became Christ-bearers. They knew that they had united themselves in the universe with what is called in the *Gospel of Saint John* the Logos, or the Word (this is not said in an historical sense, but in anti-cipation); they had united themselves with That out of which all things were made, and without which not any-thing was made that was made. Thus in those ancient times the Christ Mystery was separated from man, as it were, by an abyss; and man crossed the abyss by becoming able, through self-knowledge, to go out of himself and to unite himself with his God—to become a bearer of his God.

Let us suppose now hypothetically, in order to help us forward, that the Mystery of Golgotha had not taken place on earth, that the earth evolution had continued to the pres-ent time without the Event of Golgotha ever having taken place. Only by means of such contra-hypotheses is it possi-ble to grasp the significance of such an event as the Mystery of Golgotha. Therefore, let us suppose that this Event had not occurred up to our present day. What would have taken the place of that content which individuals found within themselves as a result of the ancient Mysteries? The man of today would be able to understand the Greek apollonian maxim, ''Know thou thyself!''; he could intend to live up to it. He could try—because, after all, the traditions have been preserved—to go through the same method of initiation as, let us say, the Egypto-Chaldean initiation of a king: that is, he could try to rise through the four stages, just as they were gone through in those pre-Christian times, to become a Christophorus. But in that case the human being would now have a very definite experience. If he followed the maxim, "Know thou thyself!" and tried to turn inward, even to pass through the conditions of fear that were suffered in that ancient time; if then he went through the experience of transformation, the setting into motion of what had first been known in a state of rest: he would now have the experience of finding nothing in himself, of now *not* finding the being of Man in himself. That is the essential fact. Certainly the maxim "Know thou thyself!" is valid for a man of our time, but self-knowledge no longer leads him to knowledge of the world. What a human being with the ancient soul-constitution still had within himself, connecting him with the Being of the world; what he could not find in the outer world but had to seek as self-knowledge, in order then to have it as knowledge of the world—that inner core of the human being, which he could then take back with him into the outer world in order to become a Christ-bearer: this the human being does not find in himself today. It is no longer there. It is important to keep this in mind. People with the foolish notions encouraged by the so-called science of our time have the idea that man is Man. A contemporary Englishman or Frenchman or German is Man just as the ancient Egyptian was. But in the light of real knowledge, that is nonsense, absolute nonsense. For when the ancient Egyptian turned inward in obedience to the rules of initiation, he found something there that a contemporary man cannot find—because it has vanished. What could still be found in the soul-constitution of pre-Christian times, and even— more or less—in the Greek soul of the Christian era, has fallen away from man and been lost. It has vanished from the being of Man. The human organism is a different one today from that of ancient times.

Using other words, we might say: When the human being turned inward in ancient times, he found *his ego*; even though dimly sensed and not in fully conscious concepts, still he found his ego. That does not contradict the statement that, in a certain sense, the ego was first born with Christianity. Therefore I say: Even though obscurely and not in fully conscious concepts, man nevertheless found his ego. As active consciousness it was indeed first born through Christianity. Nevertheless, the man of old did find his ego. For something of this ego, of the real, true ego, remained in him after he was born. You will ask: Then does the man of today not also find his ego? No, my dear friends, he does not find it. For when *we* are born the true ego comes to a stop. What we experience of our ego is only a reflection. It is only something that reflects our pre-natal ego in us. We actually experience only a reflection of our real ego; only quite indirectly do we experience something of the real ego. What the psychologists, the soul-experts, speak of as ego is only a reflection that is related to the real ego as the image you see of yourself in the mirror is related to you. The real ego, which could be found in the time of atavistic clairvoyance, and even down into the early Christian era, is not to be found today by looking into man's own being—insofar as this being is united with the body. Only indirectly does the human being experience something of his ego: namely, when he comes into relation with other people and his karma comes into play.

When we meet another person and something connected with our karma takes place between us, then some impulse of our true ego enters into us. But what in us we call our ego, what we designate by that word, is only a reflection. And through the very fact of experiencing this ego merely as a reflection in this fifth post-Atlantean epoch, we are being made ready to experience the ego in a new form in the sixth epoch. It is characteristic of this age of the consciousness soul that the human being has his ego only as reflection, so that he may enter the coming age of the Spirit-Self and be able to experience the ego in a new form, a different form. But he will experience it in a manner that now in our time would be unpleasant. Today he would call it anything but "ego," what is going to appear to him as his ego in the coming sixth post-Atlantean epoch! People in the future will seldom have those mystical inclinations that are still experienced by some individuals today, to commune with themselves in order to find their true ego—which they even call the Divine Ego. They will have to accustom themselves to seeing their ego only in the outer world. The strange situation will come about that every person we meet who has some connection with us will have more to do with our ego than anything enclosed in our own skin will have to do with it. We are heading toward a future age in which a person will say to himself: My self is out there in all those whom I meet; it is least of all within me. While I live as a physical human being between birth and death, I receive my self from all sorts of things, but not from what is enclosed in my skin. This seeming paradox is already being indirectly prepared by the fact that people begin to feel how little they themselves really are *in* the reflection which they call their ego. I remarked recently that anyone can discover the truth about himself by reviewing his own biography—factually— and asking himself what he owes since birth to this person or that. In this way he will gradually resolve himself into influences coming from others; and he will find extraordinarily little in what he usually considers his real ego (but which is really only its reflection, as has been said). Speaking somewhat grotesquely, we may say: At the time that the Mystery of Golgotha took place, the human being was hollowed out; he became hollow. And it is important that we learn to recognize the Mystery of Golgotha as an Impulse that has a reciprocal relation to this hollowed-out condition of man. If we speak truly, we must make it clear that the hollow space in man, which indeed could be found still earlier—let us say, in the Egypto-Chaldean royal Mysteries —had to be filled up in some way. In that ancient time it had been partly filled by the real ego; but this now comes to a stop at birth—or at latest, in early childhood; there is some evidence of its presence in the first years of childhood. This hollow space has been filled by the Christ Impulse. There you have the true process.

Mystery of
Golgotha

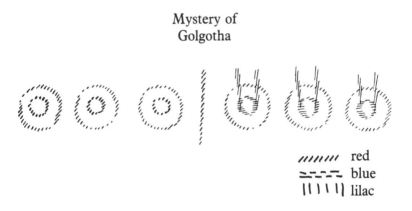

/////// red
≂≂≂≂ blue
|| | \ || lilac

Let us say, here on the left are human beings before the Mystery of Golgotha; in the middle, the Mystery of Golgotha; on the right, human beings after that Event.

Before the Mystery of Golgotha a human being had something in him that was found through initiation, as has been said. (red) Since that time it is no longer there; he is hollowed out, as it were. (blue) The Christ Impulse descends (lilac) and fills the empty space. The Christ Impulse is not to be conceived of, therefore, as a mere doctrine, a theory, but must be comprehended in accordance with facts. Only one who really understands the possibility of this descent in the sense of ancient Mystery initiation,

71

will grasp the inner significance of the Mystery of Golgotha. A man cannot today become a Christ-bearer forthwith, as he could in the ancient Egyptian royal initiation; but in any event he becomes a Christ-bearer in that the Christ descends into the hollow space within him.

Therefore, the fact that the principles of the ancient Mysteries lost their significance reveals why the Christ Mystery is of such profound importance. You will find that I have spoken of this in my book, *Christianity as Mystical Fact*. I said that what formerly was experienced in the depths of the Mysteries, what made a man a Christophorus, has been brought out on the great stage of world history and has been accomplished as external fact. That is the truth. You will see from this also that since those ancient times the principle of initiation itself has had to undergo a transformation; for what the ancient Mysteries upheld as the thing to be sought in man cannot be found there today.

People of our time have no reason to be proud that our natural science views the modern Englishman, Frenchman, German precisely as it would view the ancient Egyptian if it could. It fails completely to consider what is the essential being of man. Even the exterior human form has changed somewhat since those ancient times. But the essential change has to be understood as we have described it today. You can see from my description the necessity for change in the principle of initiation. What would a man strive toward today if he wished to obey the injunction "Know thou thyself!" in the ancient sense? What would he attain if he knew all the ceremonies and processes of initiation of the ancient Egyptians and applied them now to himself? He would no longer find what was found in the ancient Mysteries. What a neophyte in those days became at the fourth stage, present-day man would accomplish unconsciously, but would not be able to understand it. Even were he to go through all the initiation ceremonies, were he to tread all the paths that at that time led to Christophorus, he could not now approach the Christ in that way with any understanding. The man of old, when he was initiated, really became a Christophorus. But in the course of earth evolution man lost the possibility of finding within himself that Being Who became the Light-of-the-World Being. When a man of our time seeks in the same way, he finds within himself a hollow space.

However, this is not without significance in the world-process. When man loses something, he is changed because of it. Now we go through the world as human beings having that emptiness in us, but that in turn gives us special faculties. Certain ancient faculties have been lost, but through their loss new ones have been gained that now can be developed as the ancient faculties were developed for the ancient need. In other words, the path that was followed from the "gate of man" to the "gate of death" must be travelled differently today. This is connected with what I said previously: that the Spirits of Personality (the Archai) have taken on a new character, and the new initiation holds a particular relation to this new character.

In the first place, initiation came to a kind of pause in the evolution of humanity. In the nineteenth century especially, human beings were far removed from it. Only at the end of the century was it again possible to approach a real, living initiation. This real, living initiation is now being prepared, but its procedure will be entirely different from that of earlier times. I have described this earlier initiation today from a certain point of view, in order to prepare you for a deeper understanding of Christianity. What was quite impossible in earlier times—namely, to find any reality in the external world—is now a possibility through the very circumstance of our having become inwardly hollow. And this possibility will increase. It already exists to a certain extent, and may now be attained by the paths described in *Knowl-*

edge of the Higher Worlds. What is possible today is this: to acquire in a certain way a deeper view of the outer world, using the same soul-faculties (if we use them properly) with which we now view it. Natural science does not do this; its aim is limited to finding laws, the so-called natural laws, which are nothing but abstractions. If you acquaint yourselves a little with current literature, which cloaks the natural-scientific concepts in a sort of little philosopher's mantle—I might also say, puts a philosopher's little hat on them—if you make yourselves acquainted with this literature, you will see that the people who talk about these things are quite unable to relate their natural laws to reality. They reach natural laws, but these remain abstract concepts, abstract ideas. Such an individual as Goethe tried to push beyond natural laws. And what is significant in Goethe and Goethe-anism is something little understood: namely, that Goethe tried to penetrate beyond the laws of nature to the forms of nature, to nature formation. Hence, he originated a morphology on a higher level, a spiritual morphology. He tried to capture—not what the outer senses yield, but the processes of formation: what is not to be discovered by the senses, but is hidden in the forms. Thus, we can really speak today of something that corresponds to the "gate of man." We can speak of the "gate of nature-forms." I might say that there were already signs of this dawning, though still dim, when out of the chaotic mysticism of the Middle Ages such a man as Jacob Boehme[12] spoke of "the seven forms of nature." This was in his own language, and neither very clear nor very comprehensive. Nevertheless, these forms are what modern initiation must come to more and more, forms that reveal themselves within the external physical forms but extending out beyond space and time.

I have often referred to that famous conversation between Goethe and Schiller as they came from a lecture by the scientist Batsch. Schiller said to Goethe that Batsch certainly had a very splintered way of observing the world. In their day it was still far from being as splintered as that of present-day physical scientists; but nevertheless Schiller felt that it was very prosaic. Goethe remarked that of course a different method of observation could be employed, and in a few characteristic strokes he sketched his idea of the primordial plant and the metamorphosis of plants. Schiller could not grasp that and said: "That is not a matter of experience" (he meant, that is something not existing in the external world), "it is an idea." Schiller stayed with the abstraction. Whereupon Goethe replied: "If it is an idea, I am satisfied; for then I see my ideas with my eyes." He meant that what he had described was not just an idea that he only created inwardly, but that it really existed for him even though it could not be seen with one's eyes as one sees colors. That is real forming, supersensible forming (Gestaltung) in the senses. To be sure, Goethe did not develop it very far. I have told you in some of our lectures that a straight continuation of this metamorphosis of the plant and animal world—which Goethe developed only in an elementary way—brings us to a true perception of repeated earthlives. Goethe saw the colored petal as a transformed leaf, the skull bones as transformed dorsal vertebrae. That was a beginning. If someone continues with the same mode of observation, he reaches only forms, it is true, but it is the "gate of nature-forms" that he reaches; it is imaginative insight into those forms. And then he really begins to observe, not merely the skull bones that are transformed vertebrae, but the whole human cranium. He discovers that the human head is the whole human form metamorphosed from the previous incarnation, except only the former head. Of course the physical matter passes over into the earth; but the body that you carry around with you today, except just your head, the supersensible part of that form persists and becomes your head in the next incarnation. There you have metamorphosis at its highest level of development.

But you must not be deceived by appearances in precisely the modern fashion. If you deal with that kind of appearances, you will be like people who point to the passage in Shakespeare where Hamlet says in his despair, that the earthly dust of Julius Caesar must still exist; that perhaps the remains, the atoms, that once constituted the Roman emperor are now in some dog.

My dear friends, people who think in such a manner simply do not investigate the course taken by the physical organism, whether it is buried in the earth or burnt. The metamorphosis that actually takes place is the following: only the head disappears, vanishes from the earth, for it goes out into the universe; but your present body in this incarnation, except the head, is transformed, and you will find it as your head in your next incarnation. You cannot escape it. You need not consider the material substance at all. Even now you do not have the same matter in your body that you had seven years ago. You need only think of the transformation of the form. It is just as much a first stage as the "gate of man" was in the ancient sense: it is the "gate of forms." And when a man has fully comprehended this "gate of forms," he can then enter into the "gate of life," where he has no longer to do with forms, but with stages of life, elements of life. This corresponds to what I described earlier as the second stage in the ancient Egyptian royal initiation. The third stage is equivalent to entrance into the "gate of death": it is initiation into different states of consciousness. Between birth and death, of course, man knows only one; but this is one out of seven, and one must know all the various states of consciousness if one really wishes to understand the world.

Remember that you have an account of these three successive conditions in my *Occult Science, an Outline,* where they refer to cosmic evolution. You have there the seven different forms of consciousness, Saturn, Sun, Moon, Earth, and so on. In each of these stages of consciousness, Saturn, Sun, etc., there are seven life-stages; and in each life-stage, seven stages of form. What we describe as our epochs of culture—ancient Indian, ancient Persian, Egypto-Chaldean, Greco-Latin, and our present epoch—are also forms. In these we are at the "gate of forms," corresponding to the "gate of man"; out of the world of forms we can shape conceptions about the successive cultural epochs. There are seven of them in each life-stage; and when we speak of life-stages, we mean the seven successive stages of which our present post-Atlantean age is one. We are now in the fifth life-stage; the Atlantean was the previous one, the Lemurian still earlier. The purpose of these life-stages has been that man might attain the consciousness he has today. This consciousness developed out of *Old Moon* consciousness; that, out of *Old Sun* consciousness. Man's final, most perfect consciousness, he will acquire during the *Vulcan* evolution.

Thus you see how man gains a survey of the cosmos through the three successive Mystery stages. Then from this knowledge of the cosmos he acquires knowledge of man. Also from this knowledge of the cosmos he now has the possibility of bringing understanding to the Mystery of Golgotha.

Toward this understanding, today we have received, I might say, just a few incomplete ideas. But at least we have been able to grasp why, for example, the Mystery of Golgotha took place in the fourth culture-form (the Greco-Latin) of the fifth (the post-Atlantean) life-stage, and why it occurred on earth. If you read the Leipzig cycle[13] you will see how preparation was made on this earth for the Mystery of Golgotha. But all that is needed to understand the Mystery of Golgotha can be learnt from the principles of modern initiation. Thus, ancient initiation proceeded essentially from knowledge of man to knowledge of the world; modern initiation proceeds from knowledge of the world to knowledge of man.

This has been said, however, from the standpoint of initiation. You stand on one side, as it were, and on the other side you see the reflection of it. To acquire this knowledge of the world, you must start from a modern knowledge of man. I spoke recently about that. And the way we speak of ancient times must be entirely different from the way we speak of modern times. Ancient times reached knowledge of the world through knowledge of man. Speaking theoretically, we might say that what man went through as a life-process was, when completed, knowledge of the world; and with knowledge of the world in his consciousness, he could work back to man. If today you pass through forms, life, and consciousness of this world, what you really reach in this way is knowledge of man. (Look this up in my *Occult Science*.) Everything else in the knowledge of nature vanishes, and man becomes comprehensible. In the same way, from having gained knowledge of the world, man becomes comprehensible as a three-membered being (as I have shown you)— nerve-sense being, rhythmic being, and metabolic being. From man we can then pass again to knowledge of the world.

These are not contradictions. You will find such apparent contradictions at every step if you intend to enter the world of truth! If you want dogmatism, you will not be able to accept the contradictions, for they make you uncomfortable. If you want dogmatism, you can find it in one place or another; but it will never give you an understanding of reality, only something to swear by when you need it. If you want to understand reality, then you must realize that it has to be presented from various sides. From the standpoint of life, the man of old had to proceed from the world to man; modern man must go from man to the world. From the standpoint of knowledge, ancient man went from man to the world; modern man must go from the world to man. That is a matter of necessity. It is also uncomfortable for a man of modern times, but everyone must now make his way through a state of instability, a state of uncertainty. Remember how in the second stage of the Egyptian royal initiation a man came into a state of mobility, of rotation. In our time, if a man really strives to reach life through forms, he must be able to say to himself: Even if I hold concepts ever so beautiful from this or that traditional religious confession, they may be quite fine, but I still do not attain reality by means of them unless I can also set the opposite concept before me.

I have called your attention to the fact that the Mystery of Golgotha itself makes it necessary to have the two opposite concepts, so that you may say to yourself: It was truly an evil deed when men murdered the God Who was embodied in a man; but in reality that very deed was the starting-point of Christianity. For if the murder on Golgotha had not occurred, Christianity in its reality would not exist. This paradox relating to a supersensible fact may be an example of many paradoxes with which you must come to terms if you really want to attain a comprehension of the supersensible world. For it cannot be otherwise. Earlier, fear was required. Now, it is necessary to cross the abyss that gives us the feeling of standing in the universe without any center of gravity. But this must be gone through, so that concepts may no longer be something to swear by, but may be regarded as something that illuminates things from various sides—like pictures taken of a tree from various sides. The dogmatist, the scientist, the theologian believe that they can grasp the whole of reality by means of dogmas of some sort. Someone who stands within reality knows that any assertion coming from dogmas may be likened to a photograph taken from one side, giving only one aspect of reality. He knows that he must have at least the opposite aspect, so that by seeing the two together he may approach the reality of the subject. More of this tomorrow.

V

In the present group of lectures I have wanted particularly to indicate that the entire constitution of the human soul is undergoing transformation. This becomes evident to anyone who observes the evolution of humanity carefully from a spiritual scientific point of view, of humanity even in historical times, which is what we have been chiefly considering. People's way of comprehending their conception of the world, their impulses to act: everything pertaining to the human soul-constitution is changing in such a way that the slightest idea of it is beyond the understanding of external science. For science works in this realm with utterly inadequate means. Yesterday we tried to show that especially what may be called the center of human soul-life, real ego-consciousness, appears to more intimate observation to have been entirely different in ancient times from the ego-consciousness of later epochs, and that again from our present. I tried to characterize these differences by saying that in ancient times, particularly the pre-Christian, man's consciousness of self still possessed elements of reality, while in our own era, which involves principally the development of the consciousness-soul, there is only a reflection of the true ego in what we consciously call our ego. I have referred to this fact in public lectures by saying that a man of our time, especially if he thinks he is a philosopher, does not arrive at the truth because he is confused by a philosophic maxim that plays a great role in today's world view, a role that is becoming disastrous, namely, the maxim "I think, therefore I am." This Augustinian and Descartian maxim is not true for present-day man. The true form should now be: "I think, therefore I am not." A human being in our time should be fully conscious of the fact that in all he includes in the word "I" or "I am," in all he holds in his consciousness when he observes his inner soul-being, he possesses only a reflection. This reflection even includes all the concepts directly connected with his ego, concepts that must be worked through by his ego. As humanity of this present age we no longer have anything of reality in our inner soul-life. The reality, our true being, only shines into us—I explained yesterday how it shines in—and what we bear within us is merely the reflection. This fact will only become clear when we inquire into the science of initiation and observe the difference between the way a human being in ancient times could penetrate into the supersensible worlds on paths of supersensible training, and the way this is accomplished in our day. We will then be able to see that as we move on from the present into the future the paths into the supersensible world will be completely different from those of ancient times. This is especially what I wanted to make clear yesterday.

Some time ago I pointed to the objective fact underlying this whole evolution. I pointed out that if we ask what impulses, what forces are active in the evolution of the earth and the evolution of humanity, we learn that certain divine-spiritual Beings are active whom the Bible calls the Creators, the Elohim. (One could just as well take their title from another source.) We call them the Spirits of Form. I have shown, however, from various points of view that these Spirits of Form have to a certain extent—if I may use a trivial expression—finished playing their role on behalf of the most important concerns of mankind, and that other spiritual beings have taken it over.

Anyone with sufficient feeling for this fact that presents itself to supersensible research, namely, that the time-honored Gods, or God, must now be replaced in human consciousness by other impulses, will realize that indeed very much has happened in the evolution of mankind, even during historical times. Such an inner transformation of the whole human consciousness as is now taking place, and which will become more and more apparent, has certainly never occurred within historical times. As you know, I am not inclined to agree with the oft-repeated phrase: we live in a time of transition. I have often remarked that anyone can say of any time that one lives in an age of transition; and if he fancies the notion, he can consider the transition he has in mind the most important in world evolution. That is not the meaning intended in what I have said. Any time is a time of transition, but the important thing is to know what is in transition, what is undergoing metamorphosis. From other points of view other transitions may have been more significant; but for the inner soul-life of man the transition to which I am now referring, directed toward our immediate future, is the one most fraught with meaning of any in historical times.

Let us consider this further from a somewhat different point of view. When we call to mind clearly the soul-constitution in the time of ancient Greece, ancient Egypt, ancient Chaldea, it appears first of all not to have had a twofold structure as does the soul of present-day man. Perhaps we would better say that a twofold structure is now in preparation; indeed, it is in vigorous preparation, and can already be recognized in objective facts. What was formerly a mingling of soul-forces, so to speak, that worked together in the human soul, has been dividing since the fifteenth century. To a critical observer of human evolution this is quite evident. The conceptual life and the will-life were much more closely united in former times than they are now. They will separate more and more. The conceptual life, which is absolutely all we can lay hold of with our present consciousness (the ordinary, not the clairvoyant consciousness), is nothing more than a reflection of reality; and this life of conceptions also comprises all that we can grasp of our ego. On the other hand, we experience our will-life as in sleep. A man is as unconscious of what actually pulsates in his will as he is of events during sleep; but just as he knows that he has slept, in spite of knowing nothing about himself during sleep, so he knows about his will with his ordinary consciousness even though he sleeps through everything that he wills. If you have a white surface that reflects light, with some black spots on it that do not reflect the light, you see the black spots too, even though they do not reflect the light. Similarly, if you follow your life in retrospect, not only do you see your waking periods, but the periods of sleep appear in the course of your life as black spots. It is correct to say that you know nothing of yourself in sleep; but in a survey of your entire plane of consciousness the intervals of sleep may be said to appear as black spots. A person deceives himself if he thinks he knows more of his will than he does of his sleep. Man is conscious of his life of conceptions, and into this life of conceptions slip the black spots; these are the impulses of will. But man experiences these will-impulses as little as he experiences the sleep periods.

The will-life was less obscure to the consciousness of pre-Christian ancient times than it is today. Man was not so sound asleep with regard to his will; the instinctive will functioned, illuminated by the life of conceptions. On this account conceptions were not such pale reflections as they are today. Now we have on the one hand the conceptual life, which is only a reflection of reality, and on the other hand the will-life, which is a sort of sleep-condition punctuating our conscious life.

I said that what is contained in man's soul-constitution is also apparent objectively. Let us consider two phenomena that are extreme opposite poles. The rest of human life, so far as it is influenced by the human soul-constitution, resembles these phenomena. One of them is to be found to-day in the views which are especially developed in the so-called secret societies of the English-speaking peoples. (Such societies existing among other peoples, for instance, the Freemasons and similar organizations, depend entirely upon their original founding among the English-speaking peoples.) This is one extreme phenomenon. The other is to be found in the so-called Christian Church, wherever this has dogmas and rituals. These are two extreme, diametrically opposed phenomena.

There are other phenomena that are similar: for instance, what we call modern science resembles the secret-society view of the English-speaking peoples. Humanity is hardly aware that modern science is essentially similar to the views existing in these secret societies. I do not say influenced by them, but similar to them—for these things develop from different roots and then the trees become similar. It is the same with much that one finds in popular world conceptions. Today many people whose thinking does not conform to any kind of scientific world view have nonetheless similar aims. Among the scientific conceptions, philosophy alone—from an inner view—is still dependent upon the view of the Roman Catholic Church. Even the organization of man as body and soul, which philosophers regard today as unprejudiced science, is (as I have often stated) merely an outcome of the eighth Ecumenical Council of Constantinople,[14] when the spirit was abolished by the Roman Catholic Church. Thus, "unprejudiced" philosophy is nothing but the elaboration of a Church Council resolution. There are individuals who do not look at things as they are painted by the universities of our time, but who really penetrate to the facts. To them, a philosophy that accepts this dualism of body and soul, and fails to stand for the true organization of man as body, soul, and spirit, is nothing but abstract superstition originating in that Church Council—unconsciously, of course. Now if you take these two opposite views, you may find them in modified form in science and in the popular world view—as the cold of the North Pole is modified in the Temperate Zone—but if the extremes are kept in mind, the matter will become perfectly clear. You see, the secret-society view of the English-speaking people, looking up to what it considers as underlying the whole cosmic process, emphasizes particularly the so-called Architect of the worlds, the great Master Builder of the worlds. These people picture to themselves in all sorts of symbols and rites the way the great Architects of all worlds work within the cosmic process. No one recognizes that this view persists as a ghost in modern science; but it does. It is a view tending to focus exclusively upon a mere reflection of the world, upon what is only a reflection of reality.

There you have the one extreme, which takes into account only the reflection of reality and when it becomes a dogmatic world conception, it is really something entirely outside reality. That is why so much mischief can be done with these things; it is why rites and symbols, very seriously intended, or seriously proclaimed, can become a masquerade or mere ostentation. It is something a human being consciously enjoys; it gives him a lively sensation, just because it takes account of the present-day consciousness, the consciousness that is a reflection of reality, that contains the reflection of reality.

The other extreme is offered by the Church. It is radically different from the world-conception "nerve" of the secret-society view. What the Christian Church offers reckons with the other pole, the pole of the will, with those human impulses that enter the consciousness only as sleep does at night. It reckons with a reality, to be sure, but a reality that is slept through. That is the reason also for the curious development of the Christian churches, which consists in their having gradually resolved the very different concepts of ancient times into their so-called concept of faith. Anyone who knows how the followers of almost all Christian views constantly turn away from knowledge and toward faith will feel something of sleep in this practice of faith. Their desire is to prevent at all costs any clearly conscious illumination of what strives to enter the human soul from those regions where sleep also originates. Therefore, what I have described as the content of the ancient Gnosis was reduced in earlier centuries to completely abstract dogmas, which were not intended to be comprehended but only to be accepted. And in Protestantism, knowledge has been reduced to a mere subjective belief, which has its special characteristic in its being based on something that cannot be proved, something beyond the province of science. There you have the two extremes that developed in the human soul-constitution as they are now related to objective facts.

Now we may ask what really underlies this splitting of the human entity into two·poles: the conceptual life, which has become a mere reflection of images; and the will-life, which has been forced down into realms of unconsciousness where it is asleep? The underlying cause is this, that in the historical evolution of humanity the impulse for freedom is struggling upward in the development of the human being. Even freedom, dear friends, is a product of evolution! Earlier times were not ready to awaken humanity to a real impulse for freedom.

This present time in which we live can be characterized on the one hand as I have just indicated: by the fact that the Spirits of Personality are replacing the Spirits of Form. Subjectively the struggling forth from the human soul of the impulse for freedom accompanies this outer, objective fact of evolution. Whatever course events may be taking externally, however chaotic all outer happenings may become, still at the same time we have in the present and the near future the struggle of the human being, in this very age of the consciousness soul (in which we have been living since the fifteenth century) the struggle of the human being to win through to an experience of the impulse for freedom. An understanding of this impulse is being sought by modern humanity, and will be sought more and more.

But this impulse can only break out of the human soul if the soul is capable of it. In earlier times freedom in its full range was not possible, for the simple reason that before the age of the consciousness soul every impulse was instinctive. Man cannot be free if he can only take into his consciousness what plays in from an instinctively conscious reality. Modern science still reckons on this absence of freedom, on inner necessity, because it is ignorant of the fact that in our consciousness as it is developed today, in the only kind of consciousness that can be developed through modern science, no real impulses can exist. (The contemporary scientific concepts show this reflection-consciousness to the highest degree.) Nothing exists in our consciousness that springs from some reality of our own body, soul, or spirit. Reality exists in it, to be sure—especially if we develop what in my *Philosophy of Spiritual Activity* I have called pure thought—but it only exists in reflection. As soon as you find yourself within a reality, you are impelled by it, for reality *is* something; even if it acts upon you quite feebly, it is an element of necessity, it constrains you, and you must follow it. This is not the case when a reflection works upon your soul, for a reflection contains no activity, no force; it is a mere image that does not urge the soul or compel it. In this age in which the consciousness tends to have reflections, the impulse for freedom can be developed at the same time. By anything else a man would be urged to do something; but when his conscious conceptions are images and nothing but images, which reflect a reality but are not the reality, there is no reality to oppress him. He is able in this age to develop his impulse for freedom. This is a mysterious fact that underlies the life of our present time. That people have become materialists in this age can be traced to their feeling, when they contemplate their inner life, that they find no reality there, only images. And, of course, everything else is sought in the sense-world. It is true that we can find no reality, either spiritual or physical, within our soul; we find only images. This was not always so; it is only true for our age. Our age is suited to develop materialism because it has become nonsensical to say, "I think, therefore I am." We should say, "I think, therefore I am not." That means that my thoughts are only images. In the act of conceiving myself in thinking, I am not, I am only an image. This being-an-image, however, is what gives me the possibility of developing freedom.

This is another fact revealed by outer phenomena to those who survey life, may I say, according to certain leit-motivs; but its truth will only be fully revealed when we again take up initiation science, true spiritual science. You must realize, however, that today whenever people are active in philosophic or scientific pursuits, they are living very much on concepts inherited from an earlier time.

This can be seen very clearly in one of the contrasting phenomena we were considering. You can observe how the secret-society ideas of the English-speaking peoples have spread over the earth; and you will find that in these secret societies what is ancient is emphasized with a certain partiality. The more the age of any rite or dogma in this realm can be played up, the more—pardon the expression—they lick their fingers with pleasure. And when someone wants especially to captivate people with some sort of occult science, he at least announces that it is Rosicrucian, or even Egyptian—but surely old; it must be something or other old. That corresponds pretty well to the fact that in those societies knowledge that has been obtained in the immediate present is not cultivated. (Some direct research is carried on, to be sure, but only according to the rules of ancient, antiquated occult science.) On the contrary, anything such as we do here—spiritual science acquired by working directly out of the impulses of the present—anything of this sort is opposed with might and main. Opposition to anything modern is the fixed tradition of these extreme phenomena. And —leaving aside Goetheanism, which is something entirely new—if one considers thoughtfully the customary, trivial natural science and its mode of conception, one knows that all the real concepts with which it works, even all ideas (not the single laws of nature, but the forms of the laws of nature) are, fundamentally, inherited concepts. The experiments contain something new, the observations also; but the concepts are new in no sense whatever: they are inherited. And when we call the attention of one or another scientist to this fact, they become really indignant, fearfully angry, and they deny this source of their concepts.

Whence, then, comes modern thought that fancies itself so enlightened? My dear friends, it is merely the child of an ancient religion! To be sure, the religious conceptions have been discarded. People no longer believe in Zeus or in Jahve —many not even in Christ—but the mode of thought from the age when Zeus, Jahve, Osiris, Ormuzd, were believed in, the manner of human thinking has remained. It is applied today to oxygen, hydrogen, electrons, ions, Herzian waves; the object makes no difference, the mode of thought is the same. Only through spiritual science can a new kind of thinking be employed for the supersensible world and for this world as well. As I have often said, Goethe provided an elementary beginning in natural science with his morphology, which consequently is also combatted by the antiquated views. With his physics too Goethe created a beginning, but the fruitfulness of that beginning is still hardly recognized. Thus people work with what is left over—

which, of course, is comprehensible. For in an age when the consciousness is filled, not with elements of reality, but with only reflected images, it is unable, if it is thrown entirely on its own resources as ordinary, everyday consciousness, to acquire much in the way of content.

On the other hand, how were the religious conceptions acquired? It is childish to suppose that the ancient theologians thought up the contents of the Old Testament, or more recent theologians those of the New Testament, in the way present-day philosophers turn out their inherited concepts. That is a childish way of thinking. What stands in the Old Testament and the New Testament, and in the other religious books of the various peoples, came from supersensible visions, but only from the very ancient supersensible visions. It was all revealed through supersensible knowledge; and as the revelations were accepted from the supersensible world, the thought-forms were accepted too. So that today a good zoologist or a good surgeon is—unconsciously—using the thought-forms, the kind of concepts, that the seer of the Old Testament or New Testament had gained in his way by his own effort. And from the visions he obtained, the seer also developed his mode of forming concepts. Naturally it angers people today when we say to them: Even though you are zoologists, or physiologists, and certainly work in a different field, you are nevertheless using the thought-forms that originated from the visions of the ancient prophets or the evangelists. In the course of the last four hundred years, since the rise of Copernicanism and Galileism, very few new concepts have been acquired, and still less concept-forms of any sort, or trends of thought. The little that has been gained is precisely what provides the foundation for again finding supersensible paths of knowledge—through the real, anthroposophically oriented science of the spirit. Therefore, as early as the eighties of the last century I indicated clearly in my introduction to Goethe's

Morphology—and I had the words printed in italics—that I considered Goethe the Kepler and Copernicus of organic science. I intended in this way to point out the path that leads directly into supersensible realms, and that starts from the good elementary foundation which he created. Thus the kind of thoughts that continue to haunt human heads today came from ancient vision, that is, from atavistic supersensible perception. During this entire evolution of human consciousness the Creators of old, the Spirits of Form, were active; they revealed themselves to the supersensible consciousness. Now it is no longer these Spirits who are revealed to one who stands within the modern life of spirit: it is the Spirits of Personality.

You may ask, what is the difference? This is shown precisely in initiation science. The modern spiritual scientist is still someone very strange to the popular consciousness, even to the general scientific consciousness, because the latter contains only a spark of Galileism, Copernicanism and Goetheanism, and even that in very elementary form, for it is still commonly dominated by the mode of thought of the ancient seers. It was the Spirits of Form who had furnished the ancient visions, who then brought to life in man the conceptions that were active in the ancient religions and even in Christianity up to the present time. These Spirits of Form, whom we call Creators, manifested themselves, to begin with, in imaginations that arose in man involuntarily. That was their initial mode of revelation; then out of the imaginations grew the conceptions of all the ancient religions. You know that imagination is the first stage of supersensible knowledge, then comes inspiration, and then intuition. All those who wanted to reach supersensible knowledge in the ancient sense started from imaginations; they had to find their way to the Spirits of Form.

Today the way has to be found to the Spirits of Personality. Here, then, is a tremendous difference. For the

Spirits of Personality do not give imaginations to whoever wants them: a man must work them out himself; he must go to meet the Spirits of Personality. It was not necessary to go to meet the Spirits of Form. Formerly a man could be what one may call favored by divine grace, because the Spirits of Form gave him their imaginations in the form of visions. Many still seek this path today, because it is easier—but it is only attainable now in a pathological condition. Mankind has evolved, and what was psychological in earlier times is pathological now. Everything in the nature of visions, everything that depends upon involuntary imaginations, is pathological in our time and pushes a man down below his normal level. What is demanded today of anyone who wishes to push forward to initiation science, or actually to initiate vision, is that he shall develop his imaginations in full consciousness. For the Spirits of Personality will not give him imaginations; he must bring the imaginations to them. And something else occurs today. When you develop, when you elaborate valid imaginations, then you meet the Spirits of Personality on your supersensible path of knowledge, and you find the power to verify your imaginations, to bring them to objectivity for yourself.

The most elementary course for the spiritual researcher today will usually be to seek imaginations from the soundest results of modern knowledge. I have pointed out that modern science is the best preparation for spiritual research, because it offers the possibility of rising to fruitful pictorial concepts, especially if it is carried on in the Goethean sense. Of course anyone can invent images that are merely fantastic; one can patch together all sorts of stuff into arbitrary imaginations. The images one makes must first be verified by the approach of the Spirits of Personality bringing inspirations and intuitions. These are really received from the Spirits of Personality. One knows with certainty that one is in communication with those Spirits, who reveal themselves to present-day humanity from remote depths of spirit; but they will remain unproductive for one unless one brings a language to them. They keep the imaginations for themselves. Earlier, the Spirits of Form placed imaginations before a person who had supersensible vision; but the Spirits of Personality keep them in their possession, and one must come to an understanding with those Spirits—just as one would with another human being with whom one should be having thoughts in common and interchange of these thoughts. One should have free converse in the same way with the Spirits of Personality. The entire inner structure of spiritual life has been changed. The involuntary character which was the basis of the ancient revelations has been transformed into an impulse which is experienced in free activity. Someone who is not superficial, who wants to find out what really can occur, will become aware as he follows world events today (perhaps at first from something quite superficial) that a new world-plan is seeking to be realized, that behind outer events something is trying to take place spiritually. This may be sensed from world-happenings, but thoughts about it are still very vague.

Especially in social life many people may have the feeling that something is trying to be realized, something wills to happen. But if one wishes to understand what it is that wills to occur, he must approach it with something that only he himself can bring to it. What I have indicated as one kind of social impulse that is needed—but only one kind, because it is not a program, but reality—has been learnt in this way. I can say, therefore, that it is not something thought out, or fashioned from some ideal (what is called an ideal today), but it is a conception of something that presses to be realized, and that will be realized. One can only put it into concepts if one has first acquired the ability to form imaginations, and then has had them verified, proved, confirmed by the Spirits of Personality who are weaving the new world-plan.

This present-day development demands of us that we strip away all that is out of date in current science, and really find our way into new thought-forms, so that in them we may reach not antiquated visions, but imaginations built up with all our will, which we may then offer to the objective process of the spiritual world and receive back verified. This is so completely, so radically different from all earlier methods of gaining supersensible knowledge that the numerous individuals who depend upon the earlier methods resist it with all their might. For something is demanded of persons seeking to gain supersensible knowledge, something that is radical, primal, elementary, that intends to penetrate to sources, something that must be reconciled with all that is, consciously or unconsciously, antiquated. That is the reason why the spiritual science presented here attaches so little value to all that is traditional. These traditional things are certainly worthy of respect, but the fact remains that we stand at the turning-point of human evolution; and we must fully recognize that the traditional is obsolete, and that something new must be won. Hence, in a spiritual science that takes today's conditions into account, there can be no thought of faith in the old sense, nor any inclination toward the so-called Master Builder of all worlds. For both pertain only to external consciousness. When one attains a consciousness that is outside the body and outside the course of life, that is really in the spiritual world, then will and conceptions flow together again into one reality. And what was mere architecture, mere form—lifeless forms and lifeless symbols—receives inner life. Empty, obscure faith becomes knowledge, concrete self-transforming knowledge. The two unite and become a living thing. This is what must be experienced by humanity. The ancient symbols and ancient rites must be felt to be out of date. The whole earlier mode of thought must be felt as something antiquated; and the rigid forms in that mode of thought must be given life.

Just think how much use is still made today of those antiquated concepts! Certainly something useful can be done with them in many fields; but humanity would become stiff and paralyzed and withered if our antiquated ideas did not yield to something else, something containing inner life. We can no longer continue to work under the symbol of world-architecture, with rigid forms, traditional symbols, traditional dogmas. Something must bring mankind and the world together, and it must be a spontaneous, living thing.

At the beginning of our Christian era, for example, it was not yet true even of Christianity that its development was founded on something living. I have often called attention to the fact that those who first wrote about Christianity did so from the standpoint of the ancient Egypto-Chaldean science. Even the dates were not historically established. Festival dates, for instance, were determined astrologically, also the dates of the birth and death of Christ Jesus. The whole Apocalypse rests on astrology. The latter was alive in ancient times, but today it is dead, it is simply mathematical reckoning. It will only come to life again when things are comprehended with living insight: when, for instance, the birth-year of Christ Jesus is not figured out by the stars, but is seen with the vision that can be gained today in the way described. With that, things come to life. There is no life today in a calculation that determines whether some star is in opposition or in conjunction with another, and so on; but there is life when the nature of the opposition is experienced, when this is experienced livingly, inwardly—not simply externally through mathematics. In saying this, no particular objection is intended to external mathematics; it can even shed light on many things—darkness on many things, too!—but it has nothing to do with humanity's real, immediate necessity. Nor can these things be perpetuated in the old way; they would bring nothing but aridity and paralysis to the development of mankind. Of course, in judging such things people are influenced by the thought that although they themselves need not become seers—for just healthy commonsense can grasp spiritual science—yet even this kind of thinking can only be acquired with effort, while on the other hand they can easily adopt the ancient traditions and methods, and still more easily believe the church dogmas.

Now we come to a fact that we have treated repeatedly from various points of view: namely, the change that is taking place in the constitution of the human soul. It indicates on the one hand the streaming forth of the revelation of the Spirits of Personality; on the other hand, it indicates the liberation within the depths of men's souls of the impulse for freedom—a fact reflected now so urgently in the great demands mankind is raising. Today's social demands can only be understood if one is able to perceive this evolution in the constitution of the human soul. Call to mind a remark I made yesterday: that people are *beginning*—at least beginning, I said—to sense their true ego when they come in contact with other people. The man of old understood "Know thou thyself!" in the external world. For supersensible cognition it is different; but the man of ancient times, when speaking of his ego, had something real in the external world, the world in which the human being lives with his ordinary consciousness between birth and death. Modern man has only a reflection of his true ego; but something of his true ego shines into him when he comes in contact with other people. Another person who is connected with him karmically, or in any other way, gives him something real. To express it radically: it is characteristic of human beings of our present age to be inwardly hollow—and we should acknowledge it. If we practice life-retrospection honestly and faithfully, we find that the influences other people have had upon us are much more important than what we ourselves have supposedly acquired. Present-day man, of himself, gains extraordinarily little unless he obtains knowledge from supersensible sources. He need not be clairvoyant. A person is driven to daily social intercourse because actually he is only real in someone else, in his relation to another person. As we approach the sixth post-Atlantean epoch, of which embryonic impulses are now present in Russia, this fact will become so potent that a current axiom will be: No happiness is possible for one individual without the happiness of all—just as a single organ in man can only function if the whole functions. In the future this will be recognized as an axiom simply because it will be a fact of consciousness. We are still far from it—you may make your minds easy!— for a long time to come you will be able to consider your own personal happiness even though it may be built upon much human misery. But that is the direction in which humanity is developing. It is simply a fact, as when a man has a cold he must cough. He finds that unpleasant. Just so, a few thousand years from now, there will be unpleasant soul-conditions aroused when a man wishes as an individual to have any sort of happiness in the world without its being shared by others. This interdependence of mankind is inherent in human evolution, and is making itself felt today in the social demands. This is simply the direction in which the human soul is developing.

In earlier times when a man looked within, he could still find something real, even in the life between birth and death. Today, materialism is actually not unjustified in this life between birth and death if we observe man only outwardly; for what the ordinary consciousness can trace within the human being in his earthly life has only to do with material facts. Supersensible facts underlie these, but, as I said yesterday, they cease soon after birth and leave a man to take a material course until his death, when the supersensible struggles forth again. It is not from mere charlatanism that contemporary scientific research is materialistic, it is from taking into account instinctively the conditions actually existing in man today. But the people do not see beyond this life between birth and death. As soon as they begin someday to see beyond it, natural research will end as a matter of course.

Man must for once dive down into this purely material life, so that, independent of it, he may gain the spiritual. Thus, to understand what is pulsating in the most urgent demands of our time, it is absolutely necessary to look into this transformation of the human soul-constitution. And it is only possible to observe it when one is willing to do so through the science of initiation.

VI

Someone may think that the events described in connection with initiation are conjured up, as it were, by initiation itself. This would be particularly incorrect for our time. What can be described as the process of initiation, especially in our time, takes place in the soul, or in the relation of the soul to the world, for the majority of people in the world today. And they know nothing of it; it occurs unconsciously. The important fact, then, in connection with initiation is this: that some individual notices in himself an increasing consciousness of something that takes place in most other people unconsciously. That is, the difference between the initiate and the non-initiate lies in the perception of processes that most people of the present time experience as a matter of course but unconsciously. Therefore, when speaking of these things we are really speaking of something that concerns everyone more or less, especially in our time.

Now I have said that from the very description of these events—that is, of what may be perceived when they are carefully followed by initiation science—from the description itself can be learnt what transformations man has gone through in the course of his development, even in historic times. We have pointed out a few features of these transformations, especially in relation to the evolution of Christianity. In our external daily life only the outer reflection of these changes is noticed, a reflection that is really hardly comprehended even by one who wants to understand and is developing the impulse in himself toward understanding.

Let us consider this outer reflection, for example, in the

development of the Christ concept during nearly two thousand years since the Mystery of Golgotha. If you are trying sincerely to understand, you will surely find much that is incomprehensible and you will have many questions calling for answers, unless you are willing to be superficial or to accept blindly some kind of dogma. But if you persevere, you will learn—it can even be learnt from external history—that when the Christ Impulse entered the world, a certain luminous remnant of the Gnosis still existed; and in the early centuries an effort was made to understand the Christ Impulse and its passage through the Mystery of Golgotha by the help of concepts acquired from gnosticism. These concepts contained much relating to things entirely alien to present-day concepts that come from the external world. They had much to say of the evolution of the world, of the place of Christ in this evolution, of what led to His descent to humanity and His union with the human being. Much was said also about the return of Christ to the spiritual world, which then was the beginning of the spiritual earth-world.[15] In short, what the Gnosis had to say about the Mystery of Golgotha was contained in illuminating—broadly illuminating—comprehensive conceptions, the heritage of the primeval wisdom of mankind. The Church saw to it in the early centuries that the concepts of the ancient Gnosis should disappear, leaving only meager remnants that tell very little. And I have indicated to you that people are endeavoring today, wherever possible, to declare a certain world conception heretical, because it is becoming inconvenient, by saying that its intention is to warm up the ancient gnosticism—by which they think they are saying something very dreadful!

Then in place of this conception of the Mystery of Golgotha there appeared another one, which recognized the fact that human concepts were becoming more and more primitive, that people were no longer able to bring to life within themselves anything of the comprehensive and illuminating teachings of the Gnosis. I told you that what remained of the Gnosis forms the beginning of the *Gospel of Saint John*: really nothing more than a suggestion that the Christ has some connection with the supersensibly-perceptible Logos, the Cosmic Word; that the Christ as such is the Creator of all that surrounds man, of all that man experiences. But for the rest, nothing remained but the Gospel narratives; these, to be sure, are found to contain much gnostic wisdom when they are penetrated by spiritual science, but they were not interpreted according to the Gnosis. In fact, in the early centuries they were entirely withheld from believers, reserved for the priesthood only. But from them a sort of world conception was built up that included the Mystery of Golgotha, but that was based upon the increasingly abstract ideas of the so-called cultured world—ideas with little tendency toward the spiritual. People wanted, I might say, more and more simple concepts, whose comprehension required little effort. That is the reason also for the peculiar development that has come about in Gospel interpretation. While in the earliest centuries people were fully aware that the Gospels were to be interpreted out of spiritual depths, the effort was made more and more to regard them as mere narratives of the earthly life of that Being concerning Whose cosmic connection nothing more was to be admitted—at least through human knowledge—than the beginning of the *Gospel of Saint John* and a few abstractions such as the Trinity abstraction and similar ones. These were culled from abstract forms, from the ancient gnostic concepts, divested of their gnostic impulse, and given to the faithful as dogma. Interpretation of the Gospels became more and more primitive. They were to become increasingly a mere narrative

103

concerning that Being called Christ Jesus Who lived here on earth, but about Whose nature from higher, supersensible points of view people troubled themselves very little.

Then it became more and more urgent to make the Gospels also available to the public; and out of this, Protestantism arose. At first this too held fast to the Gospels. And as long as a connection with the Gospel of John still existed, a connection of knowledge, there was still a sort of bond uniting individual souls with cosmic heights—heights into which one must look if one wishes to speak of the real Christ.

But now not only the understanding for Saint John's Gospel disappeared more and more, but even any inclination toward it. The consequence was that a true relation to the Christ Impulse, to that Being Who lived in the body of Jesus, was altogether lost for later Protestantism, in fact, for all thinking Christendom. The Christ concept gradually faded away, since, to begin with, its interpretation was limited to a human narrative of the earthly destiny of Christ Jesus. The possibility completely vanished of having any concept of the Christ at all, because the subject was brought more and more into a materialistic channel. The human Jesus remained. Thus the Gospels were increasingly taken as mere descriptions of the human life of Jesus; and then the belief in immortality, in the divine nature, and so on, was attached to this description in very abstract form. (I spoke about the concept of belief yesterday.) It is not surprising that it gradually came about that people knew very little when the concept "Christ Jesus" was brought up. Christ was placed on one side, so to speak, and Jesus on the other, as synonyms signifying the same thing.[16] And what was the inevitable consequence? It was this, that finally this description of the mere earthly life of Jesus, from which all consciousness of his connection with the Christ had vanished, also lost the essence of Jesus himself; in fact, it lost all connection with the beginnings of Christianity. For when people gradually reduced everything to the merely material Gospels, to nothing but these material Gospels, they reached the so-called Gospel criticism. And that could lead to no other result than to show that the Mystery of Golgotha and all that is related to it cannot be proved historically, because the Gospels are not historical documents. Finally the connection was lost with Jesus himself. Nothing could be proved, in the way proof is regarded by modern science. And since science was the authority, people—even theologians—gradually lost the Jesus-concept, because there are no external, historical, authenticated records.

Harnack, who is a Christian theologian, even a leading one at the present time, has said: All that can be written historically about Jesus (the Gospels are not historical records) could be written on half a page . . . But even what can be written on half a page—the passage from Josephus, and so forth—does not hold up before modern historical research; so there is nothing left with which to prove the starting-point of Christianity. Those who have followed the development of Christianity with modern thinking could have taken no other path than that which finally led humanity away from Christ Jesus, even from Jesus.

This emphasizes the necessity for seeking another path, a path of supersensible knowledge such as can be sought only through the modern spiritual life. For modern Gospel criticism and modern historical research can easily be brought forward to oppose all other ways of approaching the Christ Jesus today. They are in accord with the scientific conscience of our time, and cannot support the establishing of any historical event as the starting-point of the evolution of Christianity. Indeed, we have experienced in our time the strangely grotesque fact that Christian pastors (though Protestants, to be sure) such as Pastor Kalthoff in Bremen, have considered it their task to deny the Mystery of Golgotha

105

altogether as historical fact, and to trace back the origin of Christianity to certain ideas that arose from the common social attitude of humanity at the beginning of the Christian era. Although Kalthoff was a Christian pastor, his preaching did not rest upon an historical Christ as the basis of his world conception or his interpretation of life. He believed that an idea had simply developed in people's heads from premises that heads contained at the beginning of the Christian era. Christian pastors without belief in a real Christ Jesus are the inevitable result. This could not have been otherwise, for it is connected with all the evolutionary impulses of which I have been speaking during these days, especially yesterday.

It is absolutely necessary to keep in mind that the way to Christ Jesus in our time must be by a supersensible path, that this can only be pursued by a science which itself seeks supersensible methods, but which employs the scientific conscience of modern natural science.

With regard to the modern method of finding a supersensible path even to the Christ, it is well to bear in mind that up to our day transformations have occurred and have developed in the science and knowledge of initiation. For this reason I would like to allude once more to something to which I referred here, a short time ago, but from a different point of view.

We know very well in connection with these things that there needs to be understanding for the great change that occurred in more recent evolution, toward the beginning of the fifteenth century and particularly in the fifteenth century, although it was in preparation earlier than that. This is actually passed over in silence by external history. For us it marks the beginning of the fifth post-Atlantean period, which replaced the fourth, the Greco-Latin period.

Now the problem has arisen for external science (although only among a few of the more intelligent scholars), to provide an explanation for what is usually spoken of merely as the appearance of the Renaissance—and thereby characterized in a most superficial way—of the Renaissance which played its role with elemental power throughout the cultured world from the twelfth century into the fifteenth. A strange impulse, a strange longing—mentioned even by materialistic scholars—arose in the human beings themselves, that cannot be explained by external causes, but simply showed that some elemental force was heaving and surging in mankind to bring them to a certain state of soul.

It is interesting and important to note the following: In the twelfth, thirteenth, and fourteenth centuries we are still concerned with the expiring Greco-Latin period. Then the change came. At this point, then, something special had to become manifest; and what external science has discovered is exactly what did become manifest. Science took account not so much of the change as of the gradual fading-out during the twelfth, thirteenth and fourteenth centuries of the soul-state that had been characteristic of the fourth post-Atlantean epoch. Science considered this very carefully, recognizing various riddles it presented. While the Renaissance was coming into being—the usual description of it stops with the external factors—something of extraordinary significance was taking place in the soul of European humanity. It was noticed that something must be dying out. Certain things were still experienced in the soul which after a time would have to be experienced differently. There was a feeling that humanity had to hurry to experience these things if they wanted to keep step with evolution, for later, after the change, they would no longer be able to experience them.

It is this to which I referred at the beginning of today's lecture. What is occurring now subconsciously—when recognized, it is the process of initiation—is something constantly taking place, as I have said, in the vast majority of people. Through observation of the precept "Know thou thyself!", a few individuals really succeed in becoming conscious of these things. There is a great difference between this event now and what took place in the human soul as an experience of the Mysteries in the fourth post-Atlantean epoch, a greater difference than there was, for example, between that of the fourth epoch and that of the third epoch. A few days ago I characterized for you approximately what happened in the third post-Atlantean period when a neophyte passed through the "gate of man," then through the second stage, then the "gate of death," then still further until he became a "Christophorus." These events, as I described them to you, occurred subconsciously, and then through initiation could be brought up into consciousness in the great majority of people in the third post-Atlantean epoch. But for the people of the fourth post-Atlantean epoch the entire process had already become different. Actually it was not yet so very different in the first third of this new epoch, preceding the Mystery of Golgotha. (The fourth period began, as you know, in 747 B.C., and the Mystery of Golgotha occurred at about the end of the first third of it.) But then began a time—the Mystery of Golgotha was now an accomplished fact—a time in which a more significant change occurred in what took place in the subconscious, which could then be raised to consciousness through initiation. Up to the time, approximately, of the Mystery of Golgotha, in order to attain initiation and to pass through all the stages, it was necessary (with only a few exceptions) for a man to be chosen by one of the priest-sages connected with the Mysteries, who could make this choice by virtue of a certain discernment. This necessity gradually disappeared after the Mystery of Golgotha; initiation, although still oriented to the ancient Mysteries, was nevertheless adapted to the new conditions. There have always been Mysteries of this sort, which later passed over into the modern secret societies, where for the most part ancient ceremonies and processes of initiation are imitated, but only in abstract symbols, and they no longer affect people. Real initiation is less and less attained in them, because people do not penetrate to an experience of what is simply displayed symbolically before their eyes. There did occur, however, more and more extensively—and characteristically, just at the end of the fourth post-Atlantean epoch—initiations which were directed, I might say, from the spiritual world itself; that is, initiations in which the choice of the individual to be initiated was not made by a priest, but by the spiritual world itself. Naturally, it then had the appearance of being a self-initiation, because the guiding being was a spirit and not a man. (Of course, a man is a spirit too, but you know what I mean.) Thus, especially toward the end of the fourth post-Atlantean epoch, initiations very often took place under such direct spiritual guidance. I have previously pointed out that the initiation experienced in this way by Brunetto Latini,[17] the teacher and master of Dante, is to be understood as a real initiation.

You see, what Brunetto Latini related as an external occurrence of the greatest importance appears to be a tale of fiction, though a tale with a legendary character. But Brunetto Latini intended it as a description of his initiation. He describes it in somewhat the following way, and you can see how his experiences affected the whole composition and imaginative form of Dante's great poem, "The Divine Comedy." Brunetto Latini was ambassador from his native city, Florence, to the King of Castile. He tells how he was making the return journey from his ambassador's post and learned as he was approaching his native city that his party, the Guelphs, had been defeated; therefore all that had bound him to Florence had in a sense been undermined, and in his external relations he suddenly felt no ground under his feet. When such an experience is described by a man of the Dante period, we must not think of present-day conditions or of contemporary points of view. In this respect our soul-constitution has changed enormously. If in our day someone in Switzerland learns that the city of Cologne, for example, with which he has been connected for a long time, suddenly has entirely new world-relations, is governed on an entirely new basis, he does not feel—at least inwardly—that the ground has been taken from under his feet. But we must not form mental pictures of that time from our present state of mind. For a man like Brunetto Latini it was like the end of the world. His position in the world was conditioned by his connection with the world-relations of his native city. That was gone, as he learned when he approached Florence. The world in which he had worked simply no longer existed. After calling attention to these facts, he relates further that he was led into a wood, that by spiritual guidance he was brought out of the wood and led to a mountaintop which was surrounded by the whole of creation, so far as it was known to him. We perceive immediately what Brunetto Latini wishes to indicate. He had gone through life in such a way that at a certain moment when a shocking event confronted his soul, his soul-spiritual entity separated from his physical body: he went out of his physical body. He had a spiritual experience. You have here the intervention of a spiritual guide who led this man into the spiritual world, according to his karma, at a moment when he was so startled, so spiritually shocked, that the shock was able to separate his soul-spiritual entity from his physical body. Then Brunetto Latini describes how the created universe was spread out around the mountain, and how a gigantic feminine figure appeared to him on the mountain, at whose command and direction the creation round about the mountain changed and assumed other forms. We notice that Brunetto Latini speaks of this feminine figure in the way that Persephone was spoken of in the old Mystery initiations. Now the conception of Persephone had undergone a change between the time of ancient Greece and the end of the Greco-Latin period. Brunetto Latini did not describe her as the ancient Greek poets had described her, but as she existed in human souls at the end of the Greco-Latin age. Nevertheless, we may compare what an ancient Egyptian heard in initiation as the description of Isis, and what a Greek heard as the description of Persephone, with what Latini relates of this feminine figure at whose command the forms of creation transform themselves. Strong similarities are to be found here. In fact, anyone who merely observes superficially will surely assert that what Brunetto Latini says about the feminine figure and what the ancients say about Persephone is exactly the same. But it is not the same. If you look more closely, you will notice that when the ancient Greeks spoke of Persephone, or the Egyptians of Isis, they were more concerned with a description of something permeating all that is at rest, all that is enduring. Brunetto Latini's concern was to describe how a certain force, a certain impulse—the Isis impulse, the Persephone impulse—as the *impulse of Natura* (for that is what his figure is called) pervades everything, but in a way that sets it in motion, that constantly transforms it. That is the great difference.

When Brunetto Latini saw everything changing, saw *creation being transformed* at the command of the Goddess Natura, the impulse was given him to practice self-knowledge in the new way—not in the easy way described by modern mystics, but in concrete details. He describes how, after beholding this ever-changing creation, he next saw the world of *the human senses.* He gradually learned to know the human being from without. There is a difference whether we see and describe the external world which our senses perceive in ordinary consciousness, or describe what happens *in* the senses, that is, what takes place within the human being. For with our ordinary consciousness we do not enter into

111

the inner life of the senses: we only see the outer world. When we look at the senses within, we cannot describe the outer world, for we no longer see it.

In the paintings of the larger dome here in our building,[18] I have tried in a way adapted to our time—I will say more about this presently—to bring to effective expression this viewing of the inner being of man from the sense-world. The paintings will give you an idea of what is meant by "Know thou thyself!" in the realm of the senses. You will see clearly, for instance, that on the west side of the dome an effort has been made to capture the inner eye, the microcosmic element revealed in the inner eye. It is not what the eye sees outwardly, nor the physical part of the eye, but what is experienced inwardly when we are within the eye with soul-vision. This, of course, is only possible when we refrain from the ordinary use of our eyes as organs of external sense-perception, and perceive what is within them in the same way that at other moments we perceive the outer world *through* them.

Brunetto Latini experienced this somewhat differently, not as it must be experienced today. He mentions it only briefly. Then he continues to penetrate from without into the essentially human within, and reaches *the four temperaments.* Here one learns to know man in a different way. One learns how man is affected by the interaction of melancholic, choleric, phlegmatic and sanguine impulses, and how people are differentiated externally when one of these four impulses predominates. Thereby one penetrates more deeply through the realm of the senses into the inner human being. The difference between observation of the sense realm and observation of the temperaments is that when we observe the sense realm the separate regions of the senses are sharply distinguished from one another; but through the temperaments we enter more deeply into the essentially human, where more of the universal nature of man is revealed.

An attempt was made in the painting in the little dome to show at least one part, I might say, of this perception, but only one part of it, with orientation in definite directions, but again adapted to the supersensible perception of our present time.

This is the way man must press forward. You see, Brunetto Latini describes his initiation step by step. Spiritual guidance underlies it. Next he arrived in a region where a man can no longer truly distinguish himself from the outer world. When he observes the realm of his senses and the realm of the temperaments, he can still make the distinction very well; but in this next region he can do so only slightly. There his being mingles with the outer world, so to speak: it is the region of *the four elements*. Here he experiences his own weaving within earth, water, fire, and air: how he lives with these in the universe. He no longer distinguishes very clearly between his subjective self and the outer objective world. At most he still experiences a distinction with regard to the earthly element, but with the watery, fluid element, he feels already that he is swimming in a sort of All. There was still a difference between subjective and objective, but much less definite in the experience of the temperaments than in that of the physical sense organs. Of the latter he knows that they exist in man only in the physical world, not also outside it.

Brunetto Latini then describes how he went on into the region of the *planets* and passed through it. Afterward he came to the *ocean*, reaching a place that various mystics designate as the Pillars of Hercules. Now that the precept "Know thou thyself!" had brought him to the Pillars of Hercules, he went out beyond them. He was now prepared to receive enlightenment about the supersensible world. For the mystic, especially the mystic in that time of which I am now speaking, the Pillars of Hercules are the experience through which a man goes out of himself more completely

113

than through the four elements or the planets. He enters the outer spiritual world, whose concrete beings reveal themselves only at the third stage of initiation. In the first stage, which Brunetto Latini is describing here, he enters the spiritual world as a widely extending ocean, a universal spirituality.

Latini then goes on to tell how a strong temptation came to him—inevitable, of course, at this point. He describes it very concretely: how he was faced with the necessity of forming new conceptions of good and evil, because what had enlightened him about them while he was in the sense world was useless here. He then tells how he reached these new conceptions and thereby became a different man, how he became a participant in the spiritual world from experiencing all these things. We see quite clearly from his description how at that time, the end of the Greco-Latin period, the human being was led by a spiritual being out of the physical world into the supersensible world.

Let us keep this description in mind. Even in the external development of humanity it had the immensely significant effect of inspiring Dante, Latini's pupil, for the *Divina Commedia*. If we remember that what Latini described was a typical initiation, that he actually described what was taking place in the subconscious of humanity at that particular time, and that it could also be attained through a real initiation, then we will understand what existed as soul-constitution when the fourth post-Atlantean epoch was dying out.

Now it will be important to ask what changes have occurred since, within a rather brief space of time. For what I have described is not very far in the past, only a few centuries. In this short period, what changes have taken place in the experience that humanity goes through subconsciously, which rises up into consciousness through initiation? Certainly, my dear friends, the higher the stages of initiation that a man attains, the more do the important elements of the earlier stages disappear from his vision. But one must carefully consider what is significant in the first stages. For these first stages represent precisely what is taking place in the depths of the majority of human souls, even though they neither know it nor have any desire to know it through spiritual science, not to mention initiation. It is very important to give attention to the following example: I said that Brunetto Latini describes how he was brought before the Goddess Natura. Then he passed through certain stages: through the senses, the temperaments, the elements, the planets, the ocean. There, at the Pillars of Hercules, he was already at the boundary of the essentially human. Then, in the ocean, he passed over into what was spread out before him. And now there was not even the condition that had prevailed with the elements, when he could not distinguish himself. Now he had lost himself, in a certain sense, and simply floated in the ocean of existence.

The Pillars of Hercules later play a prominent role in symbolism as the pillars of Joachim and Boaz.[19] In this connection it should be noted that in the secret societies of the present time these pillars can no longer be erected in the right way. They should no longer be erected, because the correct way is only revealed in a truly inwardly-experienced initiation. Besides, they cannot be set up in space, as they are revealed in reality when the human being leaves his body.

In what has now been given, you have the pattern—if I may use a prosaic expression—the pattern of events experienced at the turn of the twelfth and thirteenth centuries, experienced also by those who went through initiation in the same way as Brunetto Latini, the teacher of Dante. This may be compared with what takes place today in the depths of men's souls. And indeed, it is not so very different. If, however, an individual in our time should wish at the first stage of initiation to approach the created universe directly, as revealed to him by the still-existing, gigantic feminine figure, the Goddess Natura, and should wish to be under her guidance, then his supersensible path only begins in the created universe.

If an individual in our time should wish to enter into the senses directly, he would be very much in the dark in this realm. He would not have proper illumination, and would be unable to distinguish anything adequately. The point is that today it is necessary to go through another experience before approaching the sense-region, for only this makes it then possible to penetrate into the sense-region in the right way. I mentioned this experience yesterday. It consists simply in the ability to see the spiritually ideal as external reality in the *metamorphosis of forms* in this world. Thus, before entering into the sense-region one should endeavor to study the metamorphosis of forms in the outer world. Goethe gave only the first elements, but he did provide the method. As I have said, further study of the metamorphosis which Goethe discovered with regard to plants, and with regard to the skeleton in the animal kingdom, reveals the fact that our head points to our previous earth-life and our limb-organization to our coming earth-life. Thus, a necessary preparation for initiation at the present time is the ability not to think of the world as a finished static formation, but to see in whatever form lies before us an indication toward another form.

At the very beginning of my book, *Knowledge of the Higher Worlds*, you will find the essential facts for developing this kind of perception in the way best suited to our time. If you follow the instructions given there correctly, you will have the experience when you meet another human being that something like a picture of his previous incarnation will flash out of his head to you. You cannot help sensing in his head something of the form of his previous incarnation. If you follow him as he walks and notice how he puts his feet down and swings his arms, or if you are facing him and observe the gestures of his arms and hands, you will get a feeling of the way his body will be built in the next incarnation. Therefore I often said in public lectures years ago: the idea of repeated earth lives is really not so bad that materialism needs to oppose it so vigorously. If only a few things were understood about the human form, the idea of repeated earth lives would not make materialism bristle with opposition. For these things are obvious. If you are a phrenologist, for example—not by profession, but with experienced insight —then by means of the skull you are really inquiring into the form of the previous incarnation; it is quite obviously the previous incarnation. We must of course extend the metamorphosis aspect, the metamorphosis view of life into this region. We must acquire—I have often spoken of this from the social point of view—such a strong interest in the individual human being that something of a sense of his former incarnation flashes out of his skull to us. This is because the skull is in a certain sense the transformed human being of the earlier incarnation, especially with regard to the forms of the face and head. Thus we acquire a view of the world that does not stop at one form. Just as Goethe did not stop at the blossom or at the green leaf, but related one to the other, so we may gain a perception that does not stop at the single form, but proceeds from form to form, with attention upon the metamorphosis.

I sought to arouse a feeling for this by applying it to our work on the pillars in the Goetheanum: in the transition from one capital to the next and on to the succeeding ones, and in the successive development of the architraves. It was all carved according to this principle of metamorphosis. Whoever looks at the sequence of the pillars in this building of ours, will have a picture of the flexible soul-attitude one must maintain toward the outer world. If someone will complete this first step which is necessary for present humanity, and which will still be necessary for a long time for future humanity, if he will find his way to a real, inner understanding of the emergence of the second column from the first—in pedestal, capital, and architrave, of the third from the second, and so on, then in this understanding he will have a starting-point from which to press forward (in accordance with present possibilities) into the inner nature of the sense-region. Thus, something connected with the present principle of initiation is preserved below in the pillars; and above in the domes, something else is connected with it. From this point, things proceed somewhat differently.

At the time of Brunetto Latini, then, a man was spared what we shall call here the metamorphosis of life, after which one enters the region of the senses. If we presented the matter in outline, we might say: in Brunetto Latini's time a man could still enter directly into the eye (let us take the eye as representative), and feel this to be the first region. Today, we have first to concern ourselves with what envelops man. The metamorphoses of life are expressed in the sheath that covers the region of the senses externally. It lies in front of the senses and we must consciously pass through it.

Also today, the human being passes through the regions of the senses, the temperaments, the elements, and the planets. Then, however, before he goes through the Pillars of Hercules into the open ocean of spirituality, he confronts a barrier. Here, (see tabulation below) something stands in the way, something is introduced that in Brunetto Latini's time did not need to be experienced.

> Metamorphosis of life
> Senses
> Temperaments
> Elements
> Planets
> + Instrument for orientation (Compass)
> Ocean

This is not easy to describe because, of course, these things belong to intimate and subtle realms of human experience. Yet perhaps it may be done by referring again to Brunetto Latini. Latini experienced, as the first sign of his guidance by a spiritual being, the information that his native city was ruined. That was, to be sure, an event that affected Latini's inner being; nevertheless, it was external as to the facts involved. It invaded him from the outer world. It shocked him so greatly that his soul-and-spirit being left his physical body. Later he described the event as something that entered his life, something that happened in his life. We may say that he described it, though not consciously, as an event of destiny that came to him.

Such an event, or a similar one, must be experienced today in full consciousness by anyone undergoing initiation. (You will find reference to this at the proper place in my book, *Knowledge of the Higher Worlds.*) But it must be an inner experience for him: not one in connection with the external world, as in the case of Brunetto Latini, but an experience he goes through inwardly, something that has a deeply transforming effect upon him. There are, of course, such events in the lives of the majority of people, but they get scant attention. Someone who truly observes his life will be able to see that there are events in it of the utmost significance, and especially one such event. Just try to look back upon such a happening in your life, not for its outer significance but for the inner change it produced. There is one thing to which attention should really be given: that is, that such events in people's lives are not taken seriously enough. They could be felt much more profoundly; they could have a far deeper and more noticeable effect in life than they do have today. A human being can reach a deeper understanding of many things in his life, simply through a kind of general thoughtfulness. If he maintains the usual human attitude, he will not get beyond a certain superficiality in his experiencing of events of the very greatest importance. For their full import cannot really be recognized by the ordinary consciousness. The human being must first go through the other stages; after he has experienced the metamorphosis of life, the regions of the senses, the temperaments, the elements, and the planets, then—having become a radically changed human being—he penetrates to his real depths. For now he has recognized that he belongs not only to the earth but to the heavenly worlds, to the planetary regions. Only now will he rightly recognize the significance of certain experiences he has had, which were of the very first importance. Only now will he understand what such an experience signifies for himself and for the world. When he has gone through all this, he will inevitably discover the most important event of his life.

When he arrives at this place, before going out into the wide ocean of spirituality, unless he is a marked egotist and knows nothing else in the world but himself, he cannot fail to consider seriously this earlier happening. Before he goes out into the ocean of spirituality, this event appears before his soul in full force—it simply thrusts itself upon him. And at this point in his inner experience it has extraordinarily great significance. It means that only now can he go out into the immeasurable ocean of spirituality. It means that through this experience he can attain a certain center of gravity. I mean to say: After he has recognized himself as a citizen of the planetary world, if—in present spiritual conditions—he should simply launch out into the ocean of spirituality, he would find himself in a sea of surging waves, would nowhere feel sure of himself, would be tossed about in all kinds of spiritual experiences, would have no inner center of gravity. He must find this inner center of gravity by really experiencing with inner intensity the most important event of all, and *in it inwardly experiencing himself*. This will not as a rule take place in a realm of mere egotism, but will be of general human significance. It can be said today, if we express the facts quite exactly: the most momentous event in a man's life, the one that while it is being experienced affects the profoundest depths of his being, must come before him at the Pillars of Hercules before he passes through them. At this point in his life he feels a very special deepening of his being. Something comes over him of which we may say that it brings the objective world into his inner being. Something comes to him that can be described as follows: Even though, in spite of this experience, he may naturally fall back occasionally into an acceptance of life in the light of his ordinary consciousness, even though he may not be able to maintain at every step in his life this newly created soul-mood, yet, once it has been experienced, there will be moments again and again connected with it. For it would not be at all good for the human being to lose this soul-mood entirely after having once experienced it. What is meant by this mood may be characterized in somewhat the following way.

In this matter, dear friends, we should be honest and admit that for our ordinary consciousness it does hold good that, however selfless a man may be, still the most important things for him, at least relatively, are those that occur inside his skin. What occurs inside one's skin is more important for our ordinary consciousness, as a rule, than what occurs outside of it. But the soul-mood that is to be created at one's entrance to the ocean of spirituality, so that it may be retained at least for the important moments of life, is the realization that there may be external things which do not concern the person subjectively at all, but in which he participates just as intensely as in the things that do concern him subjectively. Today an individual has abundant opportunity to prepare himself well, if he will, for the soul-mood indicated. For if he enters into a true understanding of nature—not a subjective study or anything of the kind—if he tries to start from this true understanding, then much of the mood is already created. But it must be produced at this stage in the way I have described. Then if the individual can have this mood, if he can experience deeply the most important event of his life just as it happened, then at least for many moments in his life he can have this mood of objectivity that I have described, in which something external can be as important to him as something within himself, in which it is *true* that something outside can be as important as something within. (Many persons make this assertion but they are deceiving themselves.) In attaining this, however, the individual has at the same time acquired a center of gravity, a direction—perhaps I could better say, a compass, that will enable him really to push out on the ocean of spiritual life. That is to say, at this point (+ in the tabulation) there must occur what may be called *becoming equipped with the instrument for direction.* Thus a man enters the Pillars of Hercules equipped with the instrument for orientation, the compass. Only then—that is, after he has had more experience—can present-day man start out toward spirituality.

You can see from the instances I have described—the initiation of Brunetto Latini, and the changes in initiation up to our time, changes which will prevail for a long period—you can see that if we want to present the nature of man in the light of initiation science, it is even possible to present it as it is undergoing the process of transformation during short periods. But all that is so described is really happening *within* man. This is the important fact characterizing the change that the human soul-mood has been undergoing in the course of these centuries. But people fail to notice this and only a reflection of it is to be seen in external life. In the age of Brunetto Latini, whose pupil was Dante, people were the same kind of Christians as Dante: the whole heavenly world passed through their souls when they felt themselves to be true Christians. In our age there is no such forward jump; we hardly move. We must therefore have the experience of a region before that of the senses, before we go out again—so that we may enter the region we had formerly known from outside, but now enter it in a different way: before detaching ourselves further from the body, enter the region changed in our being, and taking our direction from a new instrument. The outer reflection of this process has been so altered in our time that the most thoughtful people, the very ones who are equipped with the scientific consciousness of our time—which, however, lacks this compass, really does not have it—these people have lost the Christ Jesus. He can no longer be "proved" by the means that are today called scientific. And religion itself, the Christian religion, has sunk into materialism. One of the most telling examples of the tendency toward materialism in Roman Catholicism has been the establishment of the dogma of infallibility, a purely materialistic measure. I spoke of this some time ago.

Now you might say: In spite of all that, if one looks into the inner being of man, the jump forward can be seen! Man is indeed in his essential being somewhat outside the region of the senses; but on the other hand he has a sort of cavity in which the most important event of his life unconsciously exerts an influence upon his whole organism, so that his experience can then be such as I have described. For although a man may be totally unaware of it, it does have an influence upon him, and it can come to expression in the most varied ways. Perhaps one person, seven years after experiencing this event, will become an intolerable fellow, or commit all sorts of infamous deeds; another may fall in love—he need not do so immediately; or the falling in love may itself be the most important event; a third may suddenly have gall stones; and so on. When the event remains in the unconscious, the fact can come to expression in everyday life in the most diverse ways. What enters into the consciousness

123

in the way I have described appears thus in the inner being of man; in outer life it appears in such a way that besides much else (I mention only one result) he loses the Christ Jesus.

You may say: Then what appears in the inner man to a certain extent as something flowing inward from his body, has outwardly anything but a gratifying result! This, however, is only apparent. Everything in the world has two sides. From about the middle and during the last third of the nineteenth century there was theoretical materialism: the big fellow Vogt of Geneva, Moleschott, Ludwig Büchner—these were all theoretical materialists. Clifford was the first to express the opinion that the brain exudes thoughts just as the liver exudes bile. That is, Clifford saw in the formation of thoughts a purely material process: as bile comes from the liver, so thoughts come from the brain. That materialistic age saw only matter, but at least they *thought* about matter. They thought about matter, and we can look at this in two ways. In our time we can read the books of Clifford, of Ludwig Büchner, or if you like, August Comte, Vogt of Geneva, and so on. If we develop likes or dislikes from such reading, we may be fearfully angry that people see in the creation of thoughts only an excretion of the brain, and we may take it very much to heart. Very well, if we are not materialists, we may feel that way. But we may also look at it differently. We may say to ourselves: Nonsense! what Clifford and Comte and Vogt of Geneva, what they've all said about the world is tommyrot; I am not interested in it. But I will look into what goes on in the thinking process itself of Vogt and Clifford and Comte. What they tell of their thoughts—for instance, that thoughts are merely exuded from the brain as bile is from the liver— that is plain tommyrot! I shall not concern myself with what Vogt says, but with *the way he thinks*. If we can do that, something remarkable comes to light. We see that the *kind* of thinking those persons have developed is the germ of a very far-reaching spirituality. The thoughts are so terribly thin in substance because they are only reflected images, as I explained day before yesterday. They are thinner than thin because they are only images. They are so tenuous that the man must exert a tremendous spirituality to think at all, and to prevent his thoughts from sinking down and being laid hold of by the merely material element of existence. As a matter of fact, thinking is very frequently laid hold of by this material element nowadays; it does sink down. I am even convinced that the majority of today's materially-minded people, if they had not been drilled in school, and had not crammed at the universities to pass exams, and had not swallowed materialism because their professors required it as the correct world conception—I am convinced that the majority of these people would then have been spared the thinking that must be employed for the materialistic world-view. They would much rather *not* think! Most of them would rather go to the duelling-grounds or to fraternity jamborees than use their minds. And they simply repeat what they have heard. If you would once make the attempt to study all of the genuine, recognized "wisdom" relating just to matter written by the Monists—as the materialists now call themselves rather elegantly, who as members of monistic societies go about the world making long speeches—if you would study what they have actually thought, you would find it is precious little! For the most part they merely repeat what others have said. Actually only a few authorities have established materialism; the rest only repeat—for the simple reason that a vigorous effort of the spirit is necessary to sustain modern scientific thinking. The effort is a spiritual one, and is truly not exuded from the brain as bile is from the liver. It is a spiritual effort, and a good preparation for rising to spiritual things. To have thought honestly in a materialistic way, but to have done this thinking oneself, is good preparation for entrance into the spiritual world.

I expressed this once in a lecture in Berlin, by saying that someone who only reads Haeckel's books—unless he notices much that can easily be read between the lines—quickly recognizes in him, of course, a materialist of the first water. But if he talks with Haeckel, he notices that all his thinking, so far as it is materialistic, only assumes this form really on account of the prejudices of the times; that even as Haeckel is *now*, his thinking already tends toward the spiritual. I said in that lecture: We understand Haeckel correctly, therefore, when we know that theoretically, as it were, he has that materialistic soul, but that he has another soul, one that tends toward the spiritual. Here among ourselves I can say that in the next incarnation that soul will quite certainly be reborn with a strong spirituality. The stenographer who was officially employed by us for that lecture, a typical professional stenographer, wrote that I had said Haeckel had a spiritistic soul in spite of materialism!

You see, what I want to point out is that we may certainly combat what appears as a materialistic mode of thought; indeed, it cannot be combatted strongly enough, for in the very combat lies a further development toward the spiritual. But this mode of thought does contain the essence of spirituality. And with souls who today, merely under the influence of external theology, have come to a Christ concept that is totally external, or one that is utterly untrue, there are faculties developing in a spiritual direction, faculties that will impel these souls to seek a Christ concept in the future. This is not to be taken as an invitation to ease! We are not to say: Oh, well, then it will come in time, the spiritual view will come all right, for the big Vogt fellow and Clifford and the others have made good preparation. Those who know the darkness that materialism signifies must work together to combat it. For the strength used in this fight is necessary to build up the disposition to spirituality in the theoretical materialists.

You see how complicated things are, what different sides they have. Only when we try through initiation science to penetrate into the depths of the world, do we acquire a profound knowledge of the human being. Only then do we penetrate to what is working in the depths of human nature.

VII

It relates to an elementary need of every human soul that on the last day of the year our thoughts should dwell on the transitory nature of time. For this need we may well look back in self-examination to find what has entered our external life and also our soul during the course of the year. We may well cast a glance back to the progress we have made in life, to the fruits of the experiences life has offered us. From such retrospect some degree of light may fall upon feelings that made our life seem more or less worthwhile, more or less difficult, or more or less satisfactory. We are indeed never able to observe our life as if it were the life of an isolated human being; we are obliged to consider it in its connection with the world as a whole and mankind as a whole. And if we are earnestly striving for an anthroposophical view of the world, we will feel the need with particular insistence to consider our relation to the world again and again at this constant turning-point of time, this ending of one year and beginning of another.

Since, however, our present review takes place at a time when there is so much turmoil in our souls, when all that mankind has suffered in these last four-and-a-half years is still burdening us, when as anthroposophists we observe our relation to the world and to humanity against the background of unprecedented world events, then our survey of the past year takes on quite a special character.

The thoughts I particularly wish to bring you this evening may perhaps be looked upon as an insertion, irrelevant to our previous context. At the moment we are holding before our mind's eye the transitory nature of time and of events in time, and how all this affects the human soul. But as students of spiritual science we cannot forget that when we look upon time flowing by and upon our experiences during its passing, we meet with many difficulties. Those especially whose hearts and minds are given over seriously to anthroposophical thought confront these difficulties in their observation of the world.

You all know the strange experience people have who have not travelled very much in trains. As they look out the window they receive the impression that the whole landscape is moving, hurrying past them. Of course it is they themselves who are moving with the train, but they ascribe the movement to the land the train is passing through. Gradually by accustoming themselves to their situation they get the better of this illusion and put in its place the correct idea of the sights they see through the window. Now, fundamentally but in a more complicated way, we ourselves—where the affairs of the world are concerned—are in a similar situation to those good people in the train. They are deceived about what is at rest in the landscape and what is moving. We sit within our physical and etheric bodily nature that was given to us as a kind of vehicle when we left the spiritual realms to come into physical existence between birth and death, and in this vehicle we hurry through the events of this world. We observe the world by means of this physical vehicle in which we rush along the course of earthly existence. And the world as we observe it in this way is in most cases an illusory experience. So that really we may venture on the following comparison: we see the world as falsely as the man in the train who imagines the landscape is rushing past him. But to correct the illusory view of the world to which we are prone is not so easy as correcting the illusion one has while looking out of the train window.

It is at this special moment of New Year's Eve, dear

friends, when we are still within the year in which we have had to correct so many current conceptions of the world, that such a thought may enter your souls. You know what I have told you of the experiences we would have if we were to live consciously the life from childhood to a ripe age that now we live unconsciously. I have told you how the human being matures in definite life periods, so that at definite stages he is able to know certain things out of his own power. People have to give up all manner of illusions concerning the various conditions of maturity in human life—for the reasons I have just been mentioning.

There are two kinds of illusions to which we are most subject in life, illusions that impress themselves upon our minds at such a time as this, as we glance over the past year and toward the coming one. These illusions arise from our having no idea in ordinary consciousness of how we relate to certain conditions of the outer world. This outer world is not only an aggregate of things kept in order in space; it is also a succession of events in time. Through your senses you observe the outer events taking place around you, in so far as these are natural events. You observe in the same way natural events in the human kingdom. The world is engaged in the processes of becoming. This is not generally recognized, but it is so. The processes go on at a definite speed. There is always a certain speed in what is coming about. But then turn your gaze from these events to what goes on within yourself. You know how processes go on in you both consciously and unconsciously. You do not stand in the world as a finished, self-contained spatial being, but you stand within continual happening, continual becoming, within processes continually going on and continually proceeding at a definite speed.

Let us consider the speed at which we ourselves hurry through the world in relation to the speed belonging to natural events. Natural science pays no heed to the tremendous difference existing between the speed of our own passage through the world and the speed of natural events. When we compare the part of our life that is bound up with sense observation of the outer world and the drawing of our life experiences from such observation, when we consider this part of our life in its processes of arising and passing away and compare it to the external natural events toward which our senses are directed, we find that our passage through the stream of time is far slower than that of natural events. This is important for us to bear in mind. Events in nature take place comparatively quickly; we go more slowly. Perhaps you will remember that I referred to this difference when I gave a lecture at one time not far away, at Liestal, on "Human Life from the Standpoint of Spiritual Science." From birth to change of teeth takes seven years for us human beings, that is, for the development of the physical body. Then we need another seven years for the development of our etheric body. Comparing ourselves with the plant kingdom, for instance—which can be regarded for the moment as corresponding to our etheric body—we can say that it takes just one year for the plant kingdom, represented by an annual plant, to go through all the development that can be gone through in the etheric body. We human beings need seven years for what the annual plant goes through in a single year. In other words, external nature, as revealed in the plant world, hurries along seven times more quickly than ourselves. And where the etheric world is concerned, everything is subject to the laws revealed in the plant kingdom.

You will see the significance of this, dear friends, if you reflect, for instance, on how things appear when you are travelling in a slow train beside another, faster train going in the same direction. When you yourself are travelling along slowly, the speed of the other train will not seem to you as great as if you were standing still. Or if you are travelling in a train fairly fast, but one that is still going more slowly than an express train, the express will appear to you quite slow. But go just as fast as the express and you will stay beside it. Thus the picture you have of the other train changes according to the speed at which you yourself are moving.

Now, the speed about which we want to talk here, that is, the speed at which we let our etheric body flow along, has to do with much more than merely spatial relations. It has to do with our whole judgment and experience of, and our whole attitude toward, the outer world. The spiritual scientist able to investigate these matters will say: How would it be if human beings were differently organized? if, for instance, we were so organized that we needed only one year to pass from change-of-teeth to puberty? How would it be if we had exactly the same speed as everything in outer nature that is subject to the laws of etheric life? if we got our second teeth in our first year of life, and by the end of our second year were as advanced as we are now at puberty at the age of fourteen or fifteen? Well, dear friends, then in the course of our own life we would be entirely within the course of natural events in so far as they are subject to the etheric life. We would no longer be able to distinguish ourselves from nature. For in reality we are distinguished from nature through the fact of having a different speed in moving forward through the stream of time. Otherwise we would take it for granted that we belonged to nature. And one thing above all must be pointed out: if we human beings were to parallel the speed of events in external nature, we could never become ill from an inner cause. For an illness coming to man from within actually has its origin in the difference in speed of human beings from that of natural events subject to the etheric life. Thus our human life would be quite different if we were not distinguished from the outer world by living seven times more slowly.

So we look back over the year on this New Year's Eve

unaware that in our experience during the year we have fallen out of the life of the world. We first come to realize this when after having lived a fairly good part of our life, we begin to carry out repeatedly and really earnestly these New Year reflections. People who can judge these things and who practice this retrospect regularly, will agree with me out of their quite ordinary life-experience that by the age, say, of fifty, after constant practice of this retrospect, we are obliged to admit that we have never actually drawn out of the year what it is possible to draw out. In many ways we leave unused the experiences that could have enriched us. We learn seven times less than we could learn from nature if we did not go through life seven times more slowly than nature herself. Upon arriving at our fiftieth year we have to say to ourselves: Had you actually been able to make full use of each year by absorbing everything that the year wanted to give you, then you would really only need to be seven or eight years old, at the most ten or twelve; for during that much time you would have sucked out everything that has in fact taken you five decades to absorb.

But there is something else. We would never be able to perceive that the world is a material world if we had the same speed of movement. Because we do have a different speed, the world outside, moving more quickly, appears to us as material while our own life appears to us as soul and spirit. If we were to move forward with the same speed as external nature, there would be no distinction between our soul-spiritual character and the course of outer nature. We would consider ourselves part of outer nature and experience everything as having the same soul-spiritual significance as ourselves. We would be fitted into the world quite differently. When we look back over the year on New Year's Eve we are deceived by reason of our own speed being so much slower than that of the world. For although we may look back carefully, much escapes us that would not if we were proceeding at the same pace as the world. This, my dear friends, is an undertone arising from the ground of anthroposophy, that should permeate the serious mood that befits such retrospect on the part of those dedicated to spiritual science. It should tell us that we human beings must look for other approaches to the world than those that can only be found on the external path of life, for that way only leads us to illusions.

This is one illusion. In confronting the world with our senses we move much more slowly through the world than does external nature.

But there is still another illusion. It confronts us when we reflect upon all that lights up our thinking, all that lends wings to our thinking, in so far as this arises from within us. It confronts us when we observe the kind of thinking that depends upon our will. The outer world of the senses does not indeed give us what it could give us in response to our will. We have first to go to meet the things, or events come to meet us. That is different from when we grasp our concepts and ideas as they throw their faint light out of our will. This again has another speed. When we consider our soul-life in so far as it is a life of thought, though connected with our will, our desires and wishes, we find that we have a different speed from the speed of the world we are passing through between birth and death. And if we investigate the matter anthroposophically we come upon the curious fact that in our thoughts, in so far as they depend upon our will, we move much more quickly than the external world.

Thus you see that in all that is connected with our senses we move more slowly, in all that depends upon our thinking we move more quickly, than the pace of life outside us. Actually, we move so quickly in our thoughts—to the extent that they are governed by our will, our longing, our wishes —that we have the feeling, even though unconsciously, (and this is true of everyone) that the year is really much too long. For our sense perception it is seven times too short. For our comprehension through thought, in so far as thoughts depend on our wishes and longings, we have the deep unconscious feeling that the year is much too long. We would like it to be much shorter, convinced that we would be able in a far shorter time to understand the thoughts grasped from our own wishes, our own will. In the depths of every human soul there is something that is never brought into consciousness but that is working in the whole soul experience, the whole soul-mood, and coloring all our subjective life. It is something that tells us that so far as our thoughts are concerned, it would suffice us to have a year of only Sundays and no weekdays at all. For in this kind of thinking a human being lives in such a way that actually he only wishes to experience the Sundays. Even if he is no longer conscious of it, he thinks of the weekdays as holding him up; their place in his life is only as something of which he has no need for his progress in thinking. When we are concerned with thoughts dependent on our will, on our longings and wishes, we are soon finished; in this sphere we move quickly. This is one of the reasons for our egotism. And it is one of the reasons for our obstinacy about what we ourselves think.

If you were not organized, dear friends, in the way I have just described, if with your thoughts you would really follow the course of the external world and not go forward so fast—seven times as fast as the outer world, if you did not only want to use Sundays, then your soul would be so attuned to the world that your own opinion would never seem more valuable to you than anyone else's. You would be able to adjust yourself easily to another's opinion. Just think how large a part it plays in us as human beings, this insistence of ours on the value of our own opinion! From a certain point of view we always think others are in the wrong, and they only become right when we feel disposed to consider them so.

Human beings are indeed curiously contradictory creatures! On the one hand, in so far as we have senses we move much more slowly than the outer world; on the other hand, in so far as we have will in our thinking, we move much more swiftly. So our view is blurred when we look out upon the world, because we are always given to illusion. We do not realize that we have fallen away from nature and are therefore able to become ill. Nor do we realize how we acquire materialistic ideas about the world. Such materialistic ideas are just as false as the idea that the landscape is rushing past us in the opposite direction to our train. We only have these false conceptions because we are moving seven times more slowly than the world. And then also, we cherish the secret thought: if only it were always Sunday!— because, comparatively speaking, the weekdays seem quite unnecessary for the external ideas we want to form about the world out of our wishes and out of our will. Everyone has this secret thought. The human soul-attitude is not always described so truthfully as Bismarck once described it. Bismarck made a curious remark about the last Hohenzollern emperor. While expressing his opinion about what would happen to Germany because of this emperor, he said, "This man wants to live as if every day were his birthday. Most of us are glad to get our birthday out of the way with all its good wishes and excitements, but he wants a birthday all the time!" That was Bismarck's careful characterization at the beginning of the nineties of the last century. Now, it is human egotism that makes our birthday different from all other days. No one really wants to have a birthday all the time, but from a certain point of view one would like it always to be Sunday—one could easily manage with that much knowledge! And although it wears a deceptive mask, much in our mood of soul rests upon this wish of ours to have only Sundays.

In former epochs of evolution the illusions arising from

these things were corrected in manifold ways by atavistic clairvoyance. They are corrected least of all in our age. What will correct them, however, what must arise, what I ask you to take into your souls today as a kind of social impulse, is this, that we go deeply into spiritual science as it is intended here, that we do not take it as theory but in the living way I have often described. We then have the possibility within spiritual science of correcting inwardly, in our souls, the illusions originating in those two sources of error. Anthroposophical spiritual science—and let us be particularly clear about this at the turning-point of the year—is something that lets us experience the world outside us in accordance with reality, the world that otherwise one does not experience truly, due to one's going through the world too slowly. Everything depends, actually, on how we ourselves relate to things. Just think for a moment how everything does depend upon our own attitude toward the world! To become clear about these things we should sometimes hold ideas before our souls that as hypotheses are quite impossible. Think how the physicist tells you that certain notes— C - D - E, say, in a certain octave—have a certain number of vibrations, that is, the air vibrates a certain number of times. You perceive nothing of the vibrations; you just hear the notes. But imagine you were organized in such a way (this is of course an impossible idea but it helps us to make something else intelligible)—imagine that you could perceive each separate vibration in the air: then you would hear nothing of the notes. The speed of your own life depends entirely on how you perceive things. The world appears to us as it does according to the speed we ourselves have as compared to the world speed. But spiritual science makes us aware of existing reality, apart from our personal relation to the world.

We speak in anthroposophy, or spiritual science, of how our earth has gradually developed by first going through a

Saturn period, then a Sun period, and a Moon period, finally arriving at this Earth period. But naturally everything continues to be present. In the period in which we now live, our Earth existence, other worlds are preparing their Saturn period, still others their Sun period. This may be observed by spiritual science. Even now our Saturn existence is still here. We know that our earth has gone beyond that stage; other worlds have just reached it. One can observe how the Saturn stage arises. The power to observe it, however, depends upon first changing the speed in which one will follow the events; otherwise they cannot be seen. Thus spiritual science in a certain connection enables us to live with what is true and real, with what actually takes place in the world. And if we take it up in a living way—this anthroposophical spiritual science which I have described as the new creative work of the Spirits of Personality—if we do not merely take it as a work of man for our time but as a revelation from heavenly heights, if we receive the impulses of spiritual science into ourselves livingly, then the Spirits of Personality will do what is so necessary for our time: that is, they will carry us out beyond the illusions caused by our speed being different from that of the world. They will unite us properly with the world so that, at least in our feelings about the world, we will be able to correct many things.

Then we can experience the results of our spiritual scientific striving. In the course of the past year I have mentioned many of them. Tonight in this New Year's Eve retrospect I want only to remind you of something I have spoken of before from another aspect: that spiritual science, when taken up earnestly, keeps us young in a certain way, does not let us grow old as we would without it. This is one of the results of spiritual science. And it is of quite special importance for the present time. It means that we are able, however old we may be, to learn something in the way we learnt as a child. Usually when someone arrives at his fiftieth year, he feels from the standpoint of ordinary consciousness that he has lived in the world a long time. Ask your contemporaries whether at fifty they still feel inclined to do much in the way of learning! Even if they say "yes," notice whether they really do it. A lively acceptance of anthroposophical concepts and ideas can gradually confer on people of a ripe age the power still to learn as children learn—in other words, to become increasingly young in soul—not abstractedly as often happens, but in such a way that they are actually able to learn just as formerly they learnt when eight or nine years old. Thereby the effect of the difference between our speed and that of the world is in a certain way adjusted. Thereby, though we may be of mature age chronologically, our soul does not allow us to be old; our soul makes us a child in a certain sense, makes us behave toward the world as a child. When we are at the age of fifty we can say to ourselves: by living more slowly than the external world we have actually only received into ourselves what we would have received in seven or ten years if we had lived at the same pace as the world. But by remaining fresh we have kept the power to behave as we would have behaved at seven, eight, nine or ten years. That makes a balance. And —because things always do balance in the world—this brings about the other adjustment: the reducing, in a way, what has a greater speed, namely, arbitrary thinking, those Sunday wishes as I described them. This will make it possible not always to want it to be Sunday but to use the weekdays too for learning, making a school of the whole of life.

It is true that I am suggesting a kind of ideal to you, one that is strictly anthroposophical. But perhaps, dear friends, many of you will have had deeper experiences on the last four New Year's Eves than on former ones. Anyone, however, studying world events very seriously may well regard this present New Year's Eve, in comparison to the last four, the gravest of them all. It demands of us that we enter deeply into world events, uniting our thoughts with all the ideas we can grasp through our relation to spiritual science, concerning what is necessary for the world now and in the nearest future. With the help of spiritual science we should stop sleeping in regard to world events. We must become fully awake. A mere glance today will show you that people are fast asleep. Compare modern life with the life of former ages, and you will see how much it has changed for young and old alike. How does this materialistic age affect youth today in an overwhelming majority of cases? Truly, the ideals of our modern youth are no longer as fresh, as bright, as alive, as they were in earlier times. Youth has become a youth that makes demands. There is no great desire on the part of youth to direct their soul-mood to looking forward in life, to painting ideals so full of light for the future that they are able to ennoble life. Already in youth there is the wish to exploit what they find in life. But this results in the old being unable to receive what can only be suitably received during old age. Youth uses up its forces, and old age leaves the treasures of life strewn on its path. Youth is no longer sufficiently hopeful, and old age has a resignation that is not real. Today youth no longer turns to the old to ask: will the young dreams that flow out of my heart be realized? Age hardly finds it possible today to answer: Yes, they will be realized. Too frequently it says: I too have dreamt, and alas, my youthful dreams have not been fulfilled.—Life has a sobering effect upon us.

All these things are bound up with the misfortunes of our time. They are all connected with what has so profoundly shattered mankind. When you look at them carefully, however, you will feel the need for anthroposophical impulses to be deeply inscribed in your souls. For if we wish to be awake at this turning-point of the year, we must ask ourselves: What does this era really signify? What can the future bring? What can possibly evolve out of all that civilized mankind has undergone in the chaos of these last years? If we face these questions as wide-awake human beings, then another question arises, one that is deeply connected with all our possible hopes for the future of mankind. These hopes, I could also say these anxieties, have often faced us in recent years, especially when we were giving our attention to the human beings who are now four, five, six, seven or eight years old. We who are older have much behind us that can support our souls against what is coming. There was much in the past that gave us joy, a joy that will not be experienced by those who are now five or six or eight or nine.

But when we look back over the year, dear friends, on this New Year's Eve, we find nothing in the world is absolute. Everything appears to be an illusion to us, because on the one hand we go too slowly, on the other hand too quickly in relation to the world. Nothing is absolute; all is relative. And, as you will see at once, the question that arises for us is not merely theoretical, it is a very real question: When people wonder about the future of mankind, how does it look in their souls if they have no connection with the ideas of spiritual science? One can, of course, sleep; but even if one is unconscious, this implies a lack of responsibility toward human progress. One can also be awake, and we should be awake. Then that question can still be asked concerning people's attitude in general: How is mankind's future regarded by the human souls who are not able to approach spiritual science? People of this kind are only too numerous in the world. I am referring not only to the dried-up, self-satisfied materialists, but to those countless others who today would like to be idealists in their own fashion but have a certain fear of the real spiritual. They are the abstract idealists who talk of all kinds of beautiful things, of "Love your enemy," and of splendid social reforms, but who never succeed in coming to grips concretely with the world. They are idealists from weakness, not from spiritual vision. They have no desire to see the spirit; they want to keep it at a distance.

Tonight at this turning-point of time, I should like to put the following question: When a man of this kind is sincere in the belief that he lives for the spirit, when he is convinced of the creative weaving of the spirit throughout the world, but does not have the courage to meet it in all its concrete reality as it wants to reveal itself today through spiritual science: if such a man is a true representative of the whole, or even part, of the modern world, what kind of picture do we have of him? I don't want to give you an abstract description; I would rather give you one taken from the newspapers of the world, of a man whom I have already mentioned in another connection. It is a man who for the reasons just described holds back from taking up spiritual science, believing that he can attain social ideals without it, believing that he can speak of human progress and the true being of man without taking up spiritual science, a man who from his own standpoint is honest. I have often mentioned his name—Walther Rathenau—and I have pointed out what is decidedly weak about him; you will remember, however, that I once referred favorably to his "Critique of the Times." He is so eminently a type, indeed, one of the best examples of the people of our day who are idealists, people who hold the belief that a spiritual something pervades and permeates the world, but who are not able to find it in its concreteness, that spiritual reality which alone can bring healing for all that is now pulsing so destructively through the world. It would be helpful, therefore, to learn how such a man regards the present course of the world from his standpoint outside spiritual science, what such a man says to himself in all honesty. That is always instructive, my dear friends. I would like, therefore—because all of you may not have read it—to bring before our souls the message Walther Rathenau[20] has just written to the world at large.

He writes the following: "A German calls to all the nations. With what right? With the right of one who foretold the war, who foresaw how the war would end, who recognized the catastrophe that was coming, who braved mockery, scorn, and doubt and for four long years exhorted those in power to seek reconciliation. With the right of one who for decades carried in his heart the premonition of complete collapse, who knows it is far more serious than either friends or enemies think it to be. Furthermore, with the right of one who has never been silent when his own people were in the wrong and who dares to stand up for the rights of his people.

"The German people are guiltless. In innocence they have done wrong. Out of the old, childlike dependence they have in all innocence placed themselves at the service of their lords and masters. They did not know that these lords and masters, though outwardly the same, had changed inwardly. They knew nothing of the independent responsibility a people can have. They never thought of revolution. They put up with militarism, they put up with feudalism, letting themselves be led and organized. They allowed themselves to kill and be killed as ordered, and believed what was said to them by their hereditary leader. The German people have innocently done wrong by believing. Our wrong will weigh heavily upon us. If the Powers will look into our hearts they will recognize our guiltlessness."

You see here a man pointing to what Judaism and Christianity point, namely, a Providence—Who is grasped, however, in an abstract form.

"Germany is like those artificially fertile lands that flourish as long as they are watered by a canal system. If a single

144

sluice bursts, all life is destroyed and the land becomes a desert.

"We have food for half the population. The other half have to work for the wages of other nations, buying raw materials and selling manufactured goods. If either the work or the return on the work is withheld, they die or lose their house. By working to the extremity of their powers our people saved five or six milliards a year. This went into the building of plants and factories, railways and harbors, and the carrying on of research. This enabled us to maintain a profit and a normal growth. If we are to be deprived of our colonies, our empire, our metals, our ships, we will become a powerless, indigent country. If it comes to that—well, our forefathers were also poor and powerless, and they served the spirit of the earth better than we. If our imports and exports are restricted—and, contrary to the spirit of Wilson's Fourteen Points, we are threatened with having to pay three or four times the amount of the damage in Belgium and northern France, which probably runs to twenty milliards—well, what happens then? Our trade will be without profit. We will work to live miserably with nothing to spare. We will be unable to maintain things, renew things, develop things, and the country with its buildings, its streets, its organization, will go to rack and ruin. Technology will lose ground; research will come to an end. We have the choice of unproductive trade or emigration or profoundest misery.

"It means extermination. We will not complain but accept our destiny and silently go under. The best of us will neither emigrate nor commit suicide but share in this fate with our fellows. Most of the people have not yet realized their fate; they do not yet know that they and their children have been sacrificed. Even the other peoples of the earth do not yet realize that this is a question of the very life of an entire race of human beings. Perhaps this is not even realized

145

by those with whom we have been fighting. Some of them say 'Justice!', others say 'Reparation!'; there are even those who say 'Vengeance!' Do they realize that what they are calling 'Justice,' 'Reparation,' 'Vengeance' is murder?

"We who go forward mutely but not blindly to meet our destiny, now once more raise our voice and make our plaint for the whole world to hear. In our profound and solemn suffering, in the sadness of separation, in the heat of lament, we call to the souls of the peoples of the earth—those who were neutral, those who were friendly, those belonging to free countries beyond the seas, to the young builders of new states. We call to the souls of the nations who were our enemies, peoples of the present day and those who will come after us:

"We are being annihilated. The living body and spirit of Germany is being put to death. Millions of German human creatures are being driven to hunger and death, to homelessness, slavery and despair. One of the most spiritual peoples on the whole earth is perishing. Her mothers, her children, those still unborn, are being condemned to death."

There is no passion, dear friends, in all this; it is shrewd forethought—dispassionately, intellectually calculated. The man is a genuine materialist able to assess the real conditions calmly and intellectually. He entertains no illusions, but from his own materialistic standpoint honestly faces the truth. He has thought it all out; it is not something that can be disproved by a few words or by feelings of sympathy or antipathy. It has been thought through by the dispassionate intellect of a man who for decades has been able to say "this will come," who has also had the courage to say these things during the war.

It was to no avail. In Berlin and other places in Germany I always introduced into my lectures just what Rathenau was saying at the time.

146

"We, knowing, seeing, are being annihilated, exterminated, by those who also know and see. Not like the dull people of olden times who were led stupid and unsuspecting into banishment and slavery; and not by idolators who fancy they are doing honor to a Moloch. No, we are being annihilated by peoples who are our brothers, who have European blood, who acknowledge God and Christ upon Whom they have built their life and customs and moral foundations, peoples who lay claim to humanity, chivalry, and civilization, who deplore the shedding of human blood, who talk of 'a just peace' and 'a League of Nations' and take upon themselves the responsibility for the destiny of the entire world.

"Woe to those, and to the souls of those, who dare to give this blood-rule the name 'justice'! Have courage, speak out, call it by its name—for its name is Vengeance!

"But I ask you, you spiritual men among all the peoples, priests of all the religions, and you who are scholars, statesmen, artists. I ask you, reverend Father, highest dignitary of the Catholic Church, I ask you in the name of God:

"Were it the last, most wretched of all nations, would it be right that for vengeance' sake one of the peoples of the earth should be exterminated by other peoples who are their brothers? Ought a living race of spiritual Europeans, with their children and those still unborn, ought they to be robbed of their spiritual and bodily existence, condemned to forced labor, cast out from the community of the living?

"If this monstrous thing comes to pass, in comparison with which this most terrible war was only a prelude, the world shall know what is happening, the world shall know what it is in the very act of perpetrating. It shall never dare to say: 'We did not know this. We did not wish it.' Before God, in the face of its own responsibility to eternity, it shall say openly, calmly, coldly: 'We know it and we desire it.' "

Rathenau also wishes mankind to awake and to see!

"Milliards! Fifty, a hundred, two hundred milliards—what is that? Is it a question of money?

"Money, the wealth or poverty of a man, these count for little. Every one of us will face poverty with joy and pride if it will save our country. Yet in the unfortunate language of economic thought we have no other way of expressing the living force of a people except in the wretched concept of millions and tens of millions. We do not measure a man's life-force according to the grams of blood he has, and yet we can measure the life-force of a nation according to the two or three hundred billion it possesses. Loss of fortune is then not only poverty and want but slavery, double slavery for a people having to buy half of what they need to sustain life. This is not the arbitrary, personal slavery of old that was either terrible or mild; this is the anonymous, systematic, scientific forced-labor between peoples. In the abstract concept of a hundred billion we find not money and well-being alone, but blood and freedom. The demand is not that of a merchant, 'Pay me money!' but Shylock's demand, 'Give me the blood of your body!' It is not a matter of the Stock Exchange; by the mutilation of the body of the state, by the withdrawal of land and power, it is life itself. Anyone coming to Germany in twenty years' time . . ."

What now follows is once more the result of cold intellectual foresight. This is not spoken in the way people speak who are asleep when they observe world events!

"In twenty years' time anyone coming to Germany who knew it as one of the most flourishing countries on the earth, will bow their heads in shame and grief. The great cities of antiquity, Babylon, Nineva, Thebes, were built of white clay. Nature let them fall into decay and levelled them to the ground, or rounded them off into hills. German cities will not survive as ruins but as half-destroyed stone blocks, still partly occupied by wretched people. A few quarters in a town will be alive, but everything bright, everything cheerful will have disappeared. A company of tired people move along the crumbling footpaths. Liquor joints are conspicuous by their lights. Country roads are in terrible condition, woods have been cut down, in the fields little grain is sprouting. Harbors, railways and canals have fallen into disrepair, and everywhere there stand as unhappy landmarks the high buildings of former greatness falling into ruin. And all around us are flourishing countries, old ones grown stronger and new ones in the brilliance and vigor of modern technique and power, nourished on the blood of this dying country, and served by its slave-driven sons. The German spirit that has sung and thought for the world becomes a thing of the past. A people God created to live, a people still young and vigorous, leads an existence of living death.

"There are Frenchmen who say, 'Let this people die. No longer do we want a strong neighbor.' There are Englishmen who say, 'Let this people die. No longer do we want a rival on the continent.' There are Americans who say, 'Let this people die. No longer do we want an economic competitor.'—Are these persons really representative of their nations? No, indeed. All strong nations forswear fear and envy. Are those who thirst for vengeance voicing the feelings of their nations? Emphatically, no. This ugly passion is of short duration in civilized men.

"Nevertheless, if those who are fearful or envious or revengeful prevail for a single hour, in the hour of decision, and if the three great statesmen of their nations violently contend with one another, then destiny is fulfilled.

"Then the cornerstone of Europe's arch, once the strongest stone, is crushed; the boundaries of Asia are pushed forward to the Rhine; the Balkans reach out to the North Sea. And a despairing horde, a spirit alien to European ways, encamp before the gates of Western civilization, threatening the entrenched nations not with weapons but with deadly infection.

149

"Right and prosperity can never arise out of wrong.

"In a way that no wrong has ever yet been expiated, Germany is expiating the sin of its innocent dependence and irresponsibility. If, however, after calm and cool reflection the Western nations put Germany slowly to death out of foresight, interest or revenge, and call this 'justice' while announcing a new life for the peoples, a Peace of Reconciliation to last forever, and a League of Nations, then justice will never again be what it was and, in spite of all their triumphs, mankind will never again find happiness. A leaden weight will lie upon our planet and the coming race will be born with a conscience no longer clear. The stain of guilt, which now might still be wiped out, will then become ineradicable and lasting on the body of the earth. In the future, dissension and strife will become more bitter and disintegrating than ever before, drenched in a feeling of common wrongs. Never has such power, such responsibility, weighed upon the brows of a triumvirate. If the history of mankind has willed that three men in a single hour should make their decision concerning the fate of centuries and of millions of men on the earth, then it has willed this: that a single great question of faith should be addressed to the victorious civilized and religious nations. The question is: Humanity or power? reconciliation or vengeance? freedom or oppression?

"Think! consider! you people of every land! This hour is not only decisive for us Germans, it is decisive for you and us—for us all.

"If the decision is made against us we will shoulder our destiny and go to our earthly extermination. You will not hear us complain. But our plaint will be heard where no human voice has ever cried in vain."

My dear friends, this is the product of sober intellectual foresight, most assuredly not arising from chauvinism but from materialistic thinking. I have brought it to you because

150

we live in a world in which people are most disinclined, even today, to consider the gravity of the present situation. Plenty of people will celebrate this New Year's Eve not only as it has been celebrated during the last four years but also as it was celebrated before this catastrophe. And countless people will take it as disturbing their peace, as upsetting their carefree souls, if one merely draws their attention to the situation. "Oh, it won't be as bad as all that!"—though it may not be put into words, this is what is inwardly felt, otherwise people would be judging the times differently.

For how many individuals will acknowledge the truth of what we have had to repeat over and over again during these years?—years in which we have always been hearing the following: "When peace comes, everything will be just the same as it used to be, this way and that way and the other way." How many individuals are awake to what has had to be repeated so constantly: the impossible prospect of finding conditions again as people are still allowing themselves to picture them?

We are dealing here with matters that have been thoughtfully estimated. And things appear quite differently according to whether they are estimated in a spirit of materialism or from the standpoint of anthroposophical impulses. From an external view the statements seem so right! But since there is no prospect of individuals responding consciously to what Walther Rathenau has brought forward as a last-moment expedient—namely, that the peoples should consult their conscience—alas, this talk of conscience!—what can one say? it will certainly not be consulted! Outwardly that is the way events will happen.

One can see only one hope as one looks back at how this was all prepared in the past, certainly not by any particular nation but by the whole of civilized mankind. There is just one hope: to look back on this New Year's Eve to a great universal picture, to what has previously been experienced

151

by mankind; to realize that in a certain sense men have now become sufficiently mature to bring this to an end; and to accept what the new Spirits of Personality now wish to bring down to earth from the heavenly heights. But here, dear friends, insight and will must meet. What the Spirits of Personality as new Creators are wishing to reveal will only be able to come into the world when it finds a fruitful soil in human hearts, human souls, human minds, when mankind is ready to accept the impulses of spiritual science. And what this prosaic materialistic mind has been saying about the material impulses that are actively working, is indeed correct. People should pay attention to what comes from a sober mind like Walther Rathenau—that is, the people who are asserting from a more frivolous standpoint what our times are going to bring forth. When people were in a state of utter intoxication and dreaming, when, if one speaks truly, they were talking complete nonsense—if they could only have looked ahead a little!—but they have stopped now, at least some of them—at that time one might have heard: Out of this war will come a new idealism, a new sense of religion. How often I have heard this! And it was being written over and over again, especially by professors, even professors of theology. You don't even have to go very far; it doesn't even have to be Sunday for you to find in less than ten minutes a theological professor announcing wise prophecies of this kind. But people are already talking differently. Some who have come to the top are saying that now a time of healthy atheism may well be coming, and mankind will be cured of the religion-game instigated in recent times so particularly by the poets and writers. Such opinions are already forthcoming. And they come from persons who should be listening to some of the things a man is saying who is able to judge soberly how reality is taking shape.

In response to all this one can only say: World affairs would indeed develop as we have just heard if only materialistic impulses were working in the world, in human heads and human hearts! If this were actually the case, truly not only Germany, Middle Europe and Russia would be in chains of frightful slavery but the whole civilized world would gradually be similarly enchained, never to know happiness again. For it is what has come from the past that has now made the world come to an end! New impulses do not come from that source. New impulses come from the spiritual world. They do not come, however, unless human beings go to meet them, unless they receive them with a free will. Deliverance can only come when there are human souls ready to meet the spirit, the spirit that will reveal itself in a new way through the Spirits of Personality. There must be human souls who will become creative through these very Time Spirits. There is no other way out. There are only two ways to be honest: either to speak as Walther Rathenau has spoken, or to point to the necessity of turning toward the spiritual world.

The latter way will be the subject of our New Year's Day reflections tomorrow.

Our survey on this New Year's Eve is not meant to be a mere comfortable transition into the new year. It should not be—for anyone who is awake. It should be taken in all earnestness. It should make us aware of what is lying in the womb of time if the Spirit-Child is not to be given its place there. A true perspective of the new year can only be experienced in the light of the spirit. Let us try at this moment between now and tomorrow to tune our souls to this serious mood. Tonight I would conclude only with an earnest word of direction. I myself do not yet wish to show you the actual way; I would only draw your attention to how this New Year's Eve has been received in the soul of an honest man who finds as he observes the world only material powers holding sway. It must be so regarded by the heads, the hearts, the minds and souls—if sincere—of those who do not want to turn to the spirit. There are others, also materialists, who are not sincere; they are sleeping, because then they do not need to admit their insincerity.

This is the view presenting itself to our retrospective vision. This is the New Year's Eve mood! Tomorrow we want to see, from a consideration of the spiritual world, what impression is made upon us by the outlook into the future, by the mood of the New Year.

VIII

A ray of light illumines the kind of retrospect we were engaged in yesterday evening if we take pains to consider the negative side of the matter. We might ask ourselves the following question—it has, of course, often been asked before—: What are the deeper impulses that brought mankind to today's catastrophic events? Particularly, and more important, what are the deeper impulses that brought mankind to the catastrophic mood that is clearly to be perceived in these events? Obviously, we are not always able to look directly into the deeper causes that underlie events in time. Our gaze must turn first to what may be said to lie more on the surface of happenings. It is then possible to describe this or that, and such descriptions will by no means be incorrect. This is not to be overlooked by someone intending to observe earnestly in the manner of spiritual science. A spiritual scientific observer certainly does not wish to say that everything is wrong. But one would like to point out that when someone observes the world today it does not suffice—at this present moment in time—to stop short at what is on the surface; it is necessary to go more deeply into conditions. In this respect there is nothing exactly new to be said today; rather, we should place before our souls all that contributes to our view of the New Year that confronts us so frighteningly.

You remember, I said recently that it belongs to the most essential, the most supremely important present-day knowledge that mankind is standing before a new revelation. This is the revelation that is to take place, from a certain aspect is already taking place, through the Spirits of Personality who—if it may be so expressed—are now rising to the new height of Creators. In the history of mankind up to the present day, we have only been able to attribute this capacity to the Spirits who in the Bible are called the Elohim, and whom we call the Spirits of Form. Thus, something creative will occur in what we can observe as we follow the events of the outer world.

Now it is characteristic of human nature that at first people will be averse to recognizing any such intervention of a spiritual element. Particularly at the present time there is no desire to understand such a spiritual intervention. The moment we do give our attention to it, we will have to distinguish between two things.

To make this more intelligible, I would like to say the following: At his investment in Rome the famous Cardinal Newman made a remarkable statement. He said that he saw no salvation for the Church except in a new revelation. This happened decades ago; since then, various reactions have been expressed at one place or another to this remarkable view of Cardinal Newman's.[21] And when one examines what has been said on the side of the Church and by those related to the Church creed, one finds a universal opinion that the talk should not be of a new revelation, but far rather of holding fast to the old revelation, that if anything is necessary it is first and foremost that the old revelation should be better understood than has so far been the case.

In the objections that were raised on all sides to this pronouncement by the Cardinal—who indeed had an intuition of the breaking-in of a new revelation—we can see how mankind opposes any such revelation. As I said, there are two things here to be distinguished. Mankind's struggle against receiving such a revelation is obviously not going to change the fact of its coming. It surges through the events in which man is entangled like a new wave of the spirit; man cannot push it back from the earth. It pours out over the earth. This is the one fact.

Let me say it this way: For some time, especially from the beginning of the twentieth century—to be exact, since the year 1899—as we human beings come and go about the world, we have been immersed in a new wave of spiritual life that is pouring into the common life of all mankind. And a modern spiritual investigator is simply a person who acknowledges this fact. He is someone who is aware that such an event has intervened in the life of mankind. This is the one fact.

The other fact is this, that people, by the very reason of their present attitude, need a certain shaking-up, a certain rousing, in order to notice that this wave is indeed pouring into their life. So there is a significant situation: on the one hand, the wave is actually pouring itself into life and is there; on the other hand, people refuse to notice it. They fight against it. And don't take what I say as mere imagery! For the centers, the coherers into which this wave discharges—in just the same way as the electric current in wireless telegraphy—in this sphere the coherers are human souls. Don't be deceived for a moment! For it is fact, that just by living on the earth as men of the twentieth century, human beings are the receiving apparatus for what pours into life as I have described. People may struggle against admitting this into their consciousness, but they cannot prevent their souls from receiving the impact of this spiritual wave. Nor can they prevent it from entering them.

This fact must be examined more closely. Various hypotheses must now be considered after our deliberations of the last weeks. If one asks what is the most important faculty of the human soul in our epoch, the answer is: intellectuality. And if today some people maintain—quite justifiably—that one should not just develop intellectuality but also other soul forces, their emphasis is insistent because a modern person does indeed feel that intellectuality is now the outstanding faculty, but that as it floods in upon him, he should not simply allow his other capacities to be stunted. It is because intellectuality does play such an important role today in this age of the consciousness soul that we are so frequently warned not to let our feelings become cramped. This is tremendously important.

But now we must gain a clear idea concerning this intellectuality. You know that I have spoken about it from the most varied points of view. Even in the public lectures I have not hesitated to say what was necessary about the intellectual element in our present age. I have shown, for instance, how the present scientific world conception makes particular use of it. This world conception has fastened its hold on people in all walks of life; everyone thinks in conformity with it even when he knows nothing at all about science. When someone experiments, even when someone simply observes, he works out the experiments and the results of the experiments, even his observations, with his intellect. Intellectuality is actively weaving and holding complete sway in the scientific world outlook to which at present mankind is so wedded. From such a standpoint, for instance, people even want to study social problems. But how does intellectuality really work into things? In my public lectures I have often raised the question: what sort of world picture is actually obtained from this scientific world conception? One finally realizes that a conception of the world acquired by the ordinary scientific way of thinking is not reality at all, but a specter, or a number of specters. This is true even of our atoms and of all ideas of the atomic world. Even those who take a more positivist stand and do not entirely subscribe to the atomic theory, persons like Poincaré, Avenarius or Mach, conceive of nature in such a way that they never arrive at reality, where nature is actually at work: they only reach a specter of nature. This relates to what I said here a few days ago, that actually the world of concepts in which we are living today in this age of the consciousness soul does not contain realities but merely pictures, reflected images. And we already accomplish very much when we abandon the superstition that when we read a scientific book or hear a scientific talk, we are learning the truth. If we are really aware of what is being imparted, we know that it is only an image, a kind of specter of reality.

In a certain sense, people today cherish inordinately, love inordinately, what lives in ideas of this kind, ideas that are ghostly images and not bound up with reality—in contrast, for instance, to Goethe's thoughts on metamorphosis. And people would dearly like to confine reality to this ghostly web of ideas. All those who talk today of a monistic world conception and the like, or in any way at all establish a positivist world conception, are actually believing in a curiously superstitious way in the importance of this ghostly web. They think that out of what is given them by modern scientific perception they should be able to produce a picture of reality. This indeed cannot be done. Thus, this ghostly kind of world-picture, which can be made by people at the present stage of human evolution, is very dear to their hearts. And souls are dominated today on the one hand by their love of an imagined world, and on the other hand by the fact that this imagined world yields only pictures. Moreover, the souls dominated in this way by their longing for ideas are the same souls that are struggling against the incoming spiritual wave that is in fact the true reality. It cannot possibly be turned aside by a mere ghostly web of ideas put forward by science. One only gains a correct view of these things when one realizes that this scientific way of thinking prepares people to reject all the truly real spiritual elements that are playing into the world. It is for this reason that they oppose, violently oppose, the wave that I said is nevertheless rolling in and spreading out and already living in men's souls.

You see, there is something in modern human beings, indeed in the very people who are the most representative, something that does not like the feel of this wave. It is breaking in upon them, and there is something in their consciousness that wants to resist it. We can make a sketch of it like this. (See Diagram.) Let this be modern man; then here (I) we have one layer of the human soul, and here (II) a second layer of the human soul. In the upper layer (II) is consciousness, modern consciousness, especially well-schooled in science. But the wave I am speaking about is pressing forward through the lower layer (I).

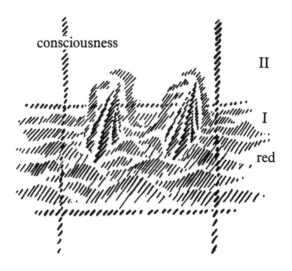

The important thing now for consciousness is that it should not simply be occupied by what becomes a ghostly web, but that it should allow what is below to flow up into it, that it should take up into itself what is there below.

If you think about this you will find something tremendously important for understanding the present constitution of the human soul. For, my dear friends, if there had not been a certain state of soul, we could never have had this terrible catastrophe of the war, or rather, the expression of this soul-catastrophe by the war. This catastrophe that is occurring in mankind takes different forms, has various aspects, and the war that has been raging for these four and a half years is only one aspect. To understand this fact of a soul-catastrophe, we must examine it minutely. One must indeed ask, what is really happening with this wave that has appeared as I have described?

This wave is still for the present below the surface of what is usually observed. One may ask, what is actually living in this wave in which the Spirits of Personality are moving? Certainly the Spirits of Personality are living in it, those Beings who want to manifest as new Creators; but also, many other things are in it. You can picture to yourselves a sea with ships moving on it, carrying the most diverse personalities travelling in this way over the waves. These may stand for us as images of the Spirits of Personality. But the waves themselves are there and they also represent something. In the sea we have, so to speak, merely the blind watery element, but this can also have its moods. And in the spiritual wave of which I am speaking, something else is present. What is flooding human souls, what is actually pushing its way into our souls, is strife, world strife. This is being enacted, one may say, behind the scenes of our modern world. Humanity is entangled in this world strife. For the spiritual investigator to perceive the Spirits of Personality is by no means an easy or comfortable matter. It is not of such a nature that one could be told: I am making you into a seer because it will give you untold happiness; you will be able to float luxuriously in spiritual perception. This would please most people. When today they are to enter the spiritual world they would like to be given something of the nature of a festive drink. They shy away if nothing is offered them that gives them a comfortable feeling of well-being. There can indeed be no question of this today. Today one feels permeated through and through by the strife going on behind the scenes of the world, a battle that must be waged, that must be placed into world evolution in the course this world evolution has to take.

It is possible to describe in various ways the form this world evolution has to take; I will mention only one. In old pre-Christian times, but gradually fading as the Mystery of Golgotha approached, it seemed a matter of course to souls who were observant, at least throughout the pagan world, that they had experiences revealing the reality of repeated earth-lives. Life in those olden days was on the whole quite different from the way modern man is inclined to picture it. Today—is it not so?—people are distinguished by whether they are educated or not. In ancient times a distinction was made between those who could observe repeated earth-lives and those who could not. But this knowledge had to recede, and I have often told you that it was the task of Christianity to hold back for a while this wave of evolution that normally would awaken in human beings a consciousness of reincarnation. In saying this, of course, one exposes oneself to all kinds of misunderstanding. Objections are put forward which if one were speaking more fully one would like, and be able, to put forward oneself. Recently somewhere or other I spoke on the subject, and then immediately received a letter asking whether I did not know that reincarnation was definitely spoken of in the Bible. Naturally you will find in my writings indications of where it may be found in the Bible; this goes without saying. But the question is not whether such reference can be found: the important fact is that in the Bible reincarnation is not openly referred to, not, one might say, held out in one's hand. It was indeed necessary in human evolution that for a time the consciousness of repeated earth-lives should recede, so that men would learn to live each separate earth-life fully and with all earnestness. Now, however, we face a reversal of the situation: we have reached the point where we can make no advance unless we turn our gaze to reincarnation. Now is the time when spiritual beings wishing to bring humanity the consciousness of repeated earth-lives have to wage a hard fight against those who would allow only old elements and impulses to enter human consciousness. This is a significant battle in which man must take part if he wants to see what is going on behind the scenes in either human evolution or the general evolution of the world.

We should not simply imagine that behind the scenes of physical existence there is a place where we can lay ourselves down to go pleasantly to sleep. That is the paradise usually pictured by the materialists. Their dearest dream is to have a really good sleep once they have passed through the gate of death. They love to imagine this because sleeping is, after all, very comfortable. But I'm sure you know that the matter is not like that. On the contrary, behind the scenes of physical existence we could not possibly entertain a desire to satisfy certain instincts in order to enhance our own personal egotism. Consequently, we become participants in a battle, a real battle.

Now the following is apparent: If people would not struggle against recognizing this battle, if they would prove themselves ready to look behind the scenes of life to what is described by the spiritual investigator, they would have a different outlook today on the whole of existence. I have always stressed the fact that we human beings should take an interest in one another. But this can only be a real interest if we let the light of spiritual science shine into our lives. Is it not true that when we enter into relation with someone—and we all do enter into relation with other people—

things happen like this: we become acquainted with people we call good, with other people whom we call neither good nor bad, and with still other people whom we call bad, who do us various kinds of harm. Certainly in external life on the physical plane we have no alternative but to relate ourselves to human beings. When someone boxes our ears and we are incited to give it right back to him in return, there is no alternative but to deal with that particular person himself. But this attitude no longer suffices for the conditions of our time. It is far more in keeping with present conditions to say to oneself: I've had my ears boxed; or someone has lied to me; this or that has been done by a human being. It is true that in physical life we have to restrict our dealings to our fellowmen, but it is important for us to realize that all kinds of spiritual forces are working in human beings with which we have to reckon. Naturally, if someone boxes our ears, we can't return it to the demon who incited him to the action; we have to deal with the man who confronts us in his physical body. However, what is so necessary on the surface of existence is not really adequate for understanding the world; it is particularly useless for grasping our social life. In other words, a person gets nowhere today if behind what goes on physically he does not fully recognize a spiritual world in its reality and concreteness. This is most important. But the majority of people are afraid of it.

Their fear is not unfounded. If you are not dull, prosaic people (of course no one here is!), a shiver will run down your spine when you think how you provide all kinds of spiritual beings with a stage for their activities. This is indeed the case. If we are conscious of the fact, we can feel that we lose ourselves in the spiritual beings who fill us out. We are like sacks stuffed to the top with all kinds of beings. Admittedly a shivery feeling is not unjustified. Nevertheless, it cannot be got rid of by denying the fact that one is such a sack—by closing one's consciousness, as it were, to become blind and deaf to what is a reality. Help must be obtained in some other way.

Now we are confronting a very significant fact. Let us assume that a man who is a human coherer into whom the wave of strife discharges but who is not inclined to acknowledge spiritual life in any way—let us assume that he gives himself up completely to the modern way of thinking, that is to say, to the thinking formed on the model of the scientific world conception. We must face these things really seriously. For at the present time unless we do so we cannot find a gleam of light, we can only succumb to Rathenau's pessimism. Take the following, for example. Suppose—shall we say—a man like Ludendorff had become a professor of botany. He would have been excellent as such; he would have done outstanding work. Indeed, he would have become quite a celebrity, as people say—so well-known that his ambition would have been satisfied. And . . . he would not have made so many human beings suffer as he has in fact done. Now Ludendorff has not had the position of a guiltless professor of botany (guiltless, that is, from a cosmic aspect, for probably he would in some way have tortured the students who were having to pass his examinations!) But let us assume he had become an innocent professor of botany, innocent from a cosmic point of view: then things would have gone quite well. But they did not go that way: he became a so-called strategist. And because of what lay within him, that is, a capacity only to think the thoughts of those ghostly webs woven by science, he could not draw up into his consciousness what discharged itself into his soul. For that way of thinking is not suited to bring up into consciousness what is discharged into the soul below. And so he became the cause of disaster for a great part of humanity. He is one of the thirty or forty individuals outwardly responsible for the present catastrophe. He is a man who from the place he occupies simply struggles against the recognition of any kind of

165

spirituality. But the time has come when persons in influential positions who fight against acknowledging the spirit, who refuse to recognize that the spiritual world is indeed playing into human life, such persons can bring calamity upon mankind. It is most important that this fact be grasped. Now, today, even if they have not held responsible positions in the war itself, still there are countless individuals who, from fear or some other reason, are resisting the wave of spiritual life that is flowing in through the Spirits of Personality—resisting it because they only want to think as science thinks.

That is the reason why today many personalities are incomprehensible, and why many are wrongly estimated. It is infinitely tragic, for example, that such a man as Ludendorff is looked upon as great. But it is true that the fact to which I have just alluded blurs people's judgment of individuals. All kinds of demonic forces play into these men, and are even imputed to them while actually they are pushing them back, because they carry in their souls a mere ghostly web on the scientific pattern and with this they cannot grasp a situation. The kind of person I have mentioned then lives his life so that in everything he does he may be insensible to the breach in his personality and to all that surges and rages deep within him. This is the case with very many people today. They are numb to what is raging within them when they attain a certain position in outer life; one cudgels his neighbor, another writes an utterly foolish book on botany, and so on; they are befogged about what is actually surging within them and causing the potential disintegration of their personality. This threatens them simply through the impact of today's inevitable events, because they are afraid of being hurled into the struggle now being enacted in the world behind the scenes, on the waves of which the Spirits of Personality wish to enter into our age.

Recognition of the spiritual world requires our being

alive to the question we are now examining. And, dear friends, it is tremendously important to take seriously what has so often been emphasized here, namely, that spiritual science should not be regarded as mere theory. If you are going to consider it mere theory, you would be better off reading a cookbook; for it is not just the content of spiritual science that is essential. The gist of the matter is how one has to think in order to do justice to spiritual science. It is a different kind of thinking from the thinking employed in the natural-scientific world of today. You see, there are definitely two ways to form thoughts. One is the dismembering, differentiating way that today plays so great a role in science, where differences are looked for, where careful distinctions are made. This is the prevailing scientific method. In science all that is said or written or done is under the influence of thinking that is dismembering, thinking that is differentiating. Exact definitions are demanded. Today when you so much as make a statement, you are nailed down to sharp definitions. But sharp, rigid definitions are simply distinguishing the things defined from the things not defined. This manner of thinking is a mask used with particular pleasure by the Spirits who are joined in this battle and who would like to tear us apart. Speaking trivially, one could say that a large number of the individuals responsible for the catastrophe of the war, or having to do with its aftermath, are really mad! But that, as I said, is speaking trivially. The important thing is to understand what has brought about the disintegration of their personalities. This first way of thinking is the thinking that is accessible to the various forces, various powers that are tearing man asunder. It must be clearly distinguished from the second way of thinking, which alone is employed in spiritual science.

The second way of thinking is a totally different kind of mental process, a completely other way of thinking. In contrast to the dismembering kind, it is a shape-forming manner of thinking. If you look more closely, if you follow what I have tried to indicate in my various books on spiritual science, you will realize that the difference does not lie so much in the content that is imparted—this can be judged from various other viewpoints; but the way of seeing the whole world and of coordinating that knowledge, the entire mode of thought representation, is a different one. This is shape-producing; it gives separate pictures, rounded totalities; it gives contours, and through contours, color. Throughout the entire presentation in the printed books you will be able to see that it has none of the dismembering character that you find in all modern science. This difference of the "how" (the mode of thinking) must be brought out just as emphatically as the difference of the "what" (the content of subject matter). Thus there exists a formative (gestaltende) way of thinking that has been developed with the especial purpose of leading to the supersensible worlds. If you take the book, *Knowledge of the Higher Worlds*, where such a path is marked out, you will find that every thought, every idea in it is based on this *formative thinking*.

This is something essential for the present time. For this formative thinking has a quite definite quality. When you dissect with your thinking, like a present-day scientist, you are thinking just the way certain spirits of the ahrimanic world think and you are making it possible for them to enter your soul. If on the other hand you exercise creative, formative thinking (gestaltendes Denken), thinking that allows for metamorphosis, I could also say Goethean thinking—represented, for instance, in the shaping of our pillars and capitals; used too in all the books I have tried to give to spiritual science—this thinking is closely bound up with the human being. Only the beings connected with the normal evolution of mankind can work creatively, sculpturally as a human being works within himself with thinking. This is

168

the amazing thing about it. You can never go astray on a wrong path if through spiritual science you engage in formative thinking. You can never lose yourself in the various spiritual beings who want to gain an influence over you. It is natural for them to permeate your being. As soon, however, as you practice formative thinking, as soon as you refrain from mere musing or from dissecting, and strive to think in the way modern spiritual science thinks, you retain possession of yourself and cannot then have the feeling of complete emptiness. This is the reason why from the standpoint of spiritual science we are always placing such great emphasis on the Christ Impulse. For the Christ Impulse stands in the direct line of formative thinking. Even the Gospels cannot be understood if they are simply dismembered. The result of that treatment is shown in modern Protestant theology, which has been pulling them to pieces: the result is that everything has fallen away; absolutely nothing has remained. The lecture cycles on the Gospels[22] follow the opposite path. They build up and shape something so that through these new forms an understanding of the old Gospels is brought about. Actually, what people need today —and this is not exaggerating in the least—is to exercise the spiritual scientific mode of thinking: then those demonic beings who are the accompanying phenomena of the Spirits of Personality on the new incoming wave will not be able to do the people harm. You see how much mankind loses by fighting against the spiritual scientific way of thinking.

I have already told you that the wave cannot be thrust aside, even if people will not go to meet it. Mankind may oppose it, may not wish to perceive it, but still the wave flows in. Then there follows what has really led to the deeper aspect of our present catastrophe, namely, the non-recognition of the spiritual world. That is finally the deeper cause of the present catastrophic events, and especially of the present tragic attitude of soul. And since it is a battle being waged in lower regions, there is no other way of experiencing this soul struggle than by developing the creativity of the human personality itself—through formative thinking. Otherwise the battle will be carried into the external world. Therefore this has to be said: that it is truly not right for people to be unwilling to examine the spiritual grounds of the present disastrous world situation. For, you notice, something extraordinarily new lies in what has been told you. It is a disclosure of the new wave that is to break upon present-day mankind through a quite special way of forming thoughts. If people give themselves up to thoughts modelled on those of science, they will simply be unable to grow to the stature required by the times. If they merely want to organize what is here in the physical world, merely want to reflect upon what surrounds them in the physical world, and have no desire for anything else to be valid, then they only destroy. And then they should not be surprised if the struggle that they do not want to fight out in the spiritual world is carried into physical life. For it has already entered humanity. If human beings will not fight it out in their souls, then it will set man against man, nation against nation, all against all. What happens here in the physical world can only be an image of the spiritual world. Either men take up the battle and fight it out in their souls—which means, they deepen themselves spiritually—or, if they persist in thinking as this present world thinks, the battle will go through their consciousness as through a sieve, and will finally end by their souls being abandoned to the external world. And this will be the cause of everything that is now going to happen. If you reflect on these things, you will realize that present-day human beings are really obliged to turn to the spirit, that this is forced upon them by world events.

Let us now consider what is presented to us this New Year's Day when we are meant to look ahead at what is coming. This particular moment offers us, indeed, a shattering prospect. What we have to keep in mind, dear friends, is this, that we must not deceive ourselves by trying to sleep through this view into the future. That is why I read you yesterday the forecast that has been pronounced by a man who calculates, who does not throw words about from sympathy or antipathy but who reckons with them. I wanted you to see where a calculating materialist of this present time finds himself. People such as he are heading in quite a different direction from a serious perception that they have to acknowledge the spiritual world simply for their own good. Whoever penetrates into the spiritual world and sees its relation to the physical world knows that certain laws prevail even when they do not seem to apply logically— when the logical consequence lies, for instance, in thinking that is dismembering, not in thinking that is formative, intuitive (anschauendes), as I have been describing. You see, laws of this kind do not prevail even externally in a rigid, letter-of-the-law way; but they are definitely there. Take such a law as this, that about the same number of men are born into the world as women. Even this law has its exceptions, even though when considered theoretically it might appear detrimental to mankind if in some particular century only a twentieth of the population born were males and all the others females! Laws do indeed exist that are not founded on ordinary logic and that can only be explained by spiritual science.

Such a law is the following: In the measure to which human beings in a certain epoch permeate their souls with recognition of the spiritual world, as I described it today, so that the spiritual world can flow into their consciousness, in the same measure can the common life of mankind also unfold and human beings be given the possibility to reach beyond their anti-social impulses and beyond all that works against true community.

But people today do not have the courage to let the spiritual world really play into their consciousness. At least a few people should know that the important need of this moment is that the spiritual world should have immediate access to human consciousness. From this point of view consider certain phenomena of this time or, I might say, favorite attitudes of this time, and you will see how people today have the desire to exclude from their consciousness any connection with the spiritual laws of existence. I showed you recently how we have to reckon with this fact even in practical matters, where a conscious connection can easily be eliminated. I was speaking at the time of intelligence tests. With these there is no longer any desire to create a direct, simple connection with the pupils' gifts; instead, in order to avoid any need for thinking, there are all kinds of external measures to test the memory and the intellectual capacity. This is also the reason why people love mathematics. Certain rules are established and the rest is mathematical reckoning. There is no need to follow the details with one's intelligence—nor would it be possible to do so. You will agree that you can picture three or four or five beans in a row, even ten beans; to imagine twenty at one glance is already difficult; but think of having to picture a thousand at one glance, or an entire million! Yet you can reckon them perfectly well, because you can make the calculation mechanically, and have no need to follow with your intelligence the details of what you are doing. What modern people particularly love is to prove something without actually having to call upon their intelligence. They find it terribly irksome if asked to follow the single stages of the proof. They prefer that the matter prove itself without human intervention. What they would like most of all is that the spiritual world would prove its own existence outside there somewhere, through spiritualism or the like. It appalls people that spiritual science should call upon them to be active at each suc-

cessive stage. That is why they love the symbols of old oc-
cultism and things of that kind—and rituals, of which they
can say: they are performed before us and we don't have to
use our intelligence to follow them; we don't have to form
the slightest conception of what is taking place. But that is
just what modern spiritual science has to insist upon: the
following up of detail. Without it, spiritual science is un-
thinkable.

It is worthy of notice that in eastern Europe we find the
seeds of what really belongs to the next epoch. All kinds of
things are being done in that eastern region that show how
the human being wants to penetrate with his intelligence
what is only meant to be encircled by a net of common intelligence. In this present age of the consciousness soul, some
people are trying to bring sharp intellectual shrewdness
down into the realm where intelligence alone should be active, where everything should simply be drawn into a net of
common intelligence. Take, for example, the way propaganda has been carried on in Russia during the last two
decades to bring about the gradual fall of czardom. Naturally this could not happen quite openly in the Russia of
serfdom and the whip. Anything written and circulated normally would have been confiscated by the police. Nor was it
possible to make speeches. And yet in a comparatively short
time, from 1900 to 1904, 60,000,000 anti-czarist pamphlets
appeared in Russia. Of these 60,000,000 the police tracked
down only twenty to twenty-five percent; the others were
distributed, and an immense number appeared just before
the downfall of the Czar. Thus a large proportion of the
population were prepared for the end of czardom. Now how
did it ever come about that, in spite of all that was scented
out and confiscated by the police, still out of sixty million
pamphlets, each one of which called for revolution and the
end of czardom, hardly a quarter were seized? The explanation is that those who led the agitation had discovered a very

definite fact, which today is of great importance but which people simply fail to investigate. When they do investigate it in an ahrimanic way, as those Revolutionary leaders did, they have something that enables them to work with tremendous power. Those leaders discovered that the same words addressed to a strictly czarist member of the police worked in an entirely different way when addressed to an ordinary man in the street. The same words that, spoken in the proper manner, sound to a policeman as gentle as a lamb can under certain conditions work upon the populace in a most extreme socialistic sense. Certainly pamphlets were not written then as they are written now in Switzerland—and immediately confiscated; but books or pamphlets were distributed about botany, about plants, that simply by the way they were written prepared souls fully, so that in 1917 Russia was completely ready for the Revolution. It is enormously important to be aware of this secret: that what one says affects one person quite differently from the way it affects another person. In any case, this has all been carefully studied, and the studies made in this sphere are thoroughly characteristic of our time. In fact, they are part of what is struggling most bitterly against the spiritual science that is entering the world.

For instance, I cannot think of anything more strongly opposed to the real essence of the spirit than such books as those by Nikolai Rubakin. Rubakin attempts to study the human soul—and in a new way, but in such a way that it completely denies everything that is alive in spiritual science: that is, in such a way that in a certain sense the intelligence is maintained as it works, but also the activity of the individual intelligence can be excluded in the working. Such a man as Rubakin is reckoning that everything that happens at the present time is bound up with intelligence, but that we should not always work through the subjective intelligence. In this sense he has made the following wide

174

investigation: he has organized a study of people who read books. He asks them to name their favorite books and to say what particularly impressed them in those books, and what kind of influence the books have had upon them. He puts these questions to them in such a way that no account is taken of their sympathies and antipathies—these are expressly ignored, so that only the objective working of their intelligence comes into consideration. The readers give themselves up to a self-analysis of such a kind that simply through the questions he asks they say things that allow him to see more deeply into their souls than they do themselves. This is one method.

The other method is this: again a questionnaire is sent to thousands and thousands of people, asking them to analyze current books. No notice is taken whether a book is on mathematics or botany or politics or socialism or anarchy; that is of minor importance, for that is merely the reading matter, and most readers are unaware that that constitutes only one part of a book. Rubakin establishes how the book works by the beauty of its phrasing, by its disclosure of the writer's temperament, or the monotony of his style. These are genuine qualities through which he can discover the prevailing objective intelligence. He establishes it statistically through these books. The whole method goes to show the outstreaming and intaking of intelligence that is active at the present time. Were such a science carried a bit further, someone could write a fearfully revolutionary book on Jupiter, and someone else a book on the right foreleg of the cockchafer, and the second book would serve the purpose of this Rubakin inquiry just as well as the first. For here it is not a question of what is said but of how it is said; from this it is learnt what works in people as objective intelligence, of which people themselves are not conscious. Here a person is not active subjectively, because he is not allowing his individual intelligence to play a part—any more than he allows it to do in arithmetic. The person is participating in a general prevailing intelligence and is not involved in what this normally brings into action in individual human beings, for his subjective intelligence has been completely excluded.

On the basis of such a science one could found a college today that would undertake to spread revolutionary propaganda simply by following the lines I have indicated. There are such endeavors at the present time. The intention of all of them is, in this epoch of intelligence not to include man in the intelligence but to throw him out of it. This comes from the same source as the desire that man shall not receive the spiritual world consciously, that is, with the consciousness belonging to this present day. But, of course, that is essential. The only salvation for mankind today and in the immediate future is that we accept boldly and courageously the coming-in of the spiritual world. We will not have to give intelligence tests or collect statistics on books and their readers to discover what wants to reveal itself that is living in humanity right now. Another way will be taken, dear friends. For what is the purpose of all this? To speak quite simply, all those endeavors of Rubakin and the rest aim at pulling man out of his skin, because in his skin he has to make use of his intelligence and, what is more, to turn it toward a spiritual life. People would like to get outside their skin. They no longer want to live in it, because they know something living is streaming into it and they find it unpleasant to make the acquaintance of this living thing; they would prefer to escape it. They would like to objectify their intelligent nature, to get outside of it and sit down beside it, so that the wave would only go through it and not through them. But that is also what spiritual science wants!—a science that is not just shut up inside the skin. We should indeed get out of our skin, but not in the wrong way as the experiments I have described accomplish it. People have that wrong urge already. In reality they should accept a

176

knowledge that simply has to be confirmed by their sound human understanding. They do not need to be free of their body to acquire a knowledge that is itself independent of what they do in their body. This is the task of truth—the other is a caricature of truth. And such caricatures of the true spiritual task of the present age are responsible for the evils of this age that have brought us to our present impasse.

When we see in this way what is dominating our epoch, we know why it is that people who do not want to acknowledge the real spirit, but who are honest and do not delude themselves, are at the same time clear about what confronts mankind if it still clings to materialism. We must realize that in this signpost pointing to the spirit lies what need not necessarily make us pessimistic. When we find how little people are inclined even today to approach the spiritual world in the way spiritual science indicates, then we see where the deeper causes of the present ruin actually lie.

Even this year all kinds of articles about Christmas have appeared in print again. One can hardly believe that such rubbish would reappear in these grave times. Everyone writes surprisingly well, in fact, quite beautifully of how people should love one another. Actually they hate one another as never before, but there it is in writing that we should love one another, we should love our enemies, and so on. There was even a letter printed entitled "A woman's letter to Walther Rathenau." People write in such a manner that, looked at spiritually, the idea lying behind the writing appears in a very strange light. They write of human love, of Christianity, of every possible thing; it is all very beautiful, and the people reading it think it is exquisite. Yet it is nothing but obsolete concept-coins rumbling around in their heads or hearts. And while all this rumbles and rolls, the writer or the reader stands behind and feels a sensuous love for these words, so that all this has the effect upon him of rich sweetmeats. One can dream so deliciously when one says: Christ preached love for one's neighbor; Christianity must blossom again; and so on. With that kind of attitude, the people feel not the slightest necessity to accept the concrete spiritual world in the innermost depths of their soul, with their whole being—as spiritual science requires. The pressing need is for us to take these things in earnest. If we recognize them theoretically and then still do nothing more than stand in reverence before Wilsonism or fall into national chauvinism, still holding forth in the old way—then we shall never get beyond this catastrophe. It will continue until human beings make up their minds really to accept the spiritual world as it must be accepted today, that is, with consciousness that is concrete and without fear or timidity.

And so when we gaze into the new cosmic year, we see on the one hand how some people, just to allay their fears, offer political forecasts and found Leagues of Nations that are to abolish war from the world. In spite of rejoicing that there will not be another Vienna Congress, people are already beginning to say that they would be content if the Congress of Versailles only procured for us as many months of peace as the Vienna Congress brought years of peace. For, in truth, men love to hold thoughts that act like narcotics. The strongest benumbing thought for people today, after they have rejected certain others, is that Wilson is the right man for the future. He is the great man, is he not?—a man who thinks fourteen abstract thoughts are able to transform life in our present world into a paradise! It is comforting, is it not?—something that can lull us to sleep. It is far less comfortable to say: If we are to be saved from a future such as Rathenau predicts, it is necessary that as many individuals as possible come to a conscious recognition of the spiritual world.

This is what one would like to bring to pass in at least a few souls after the New Year's Eve retrospect that we shared last night. One hopes that the truth of that experi-

178

ence has stirred our souls so strongly that someone can say: if mankind continues with the thinking that has become customary, not only in one people but among all the peoples around the earth, then Rathenau's forecast must be correct. Dear friends, there is no necessity for it to be correct! Mankind has the chance to prove that there is no need for his forecast to be correct. This can be our New Year resolution, that we will exert our will so that the foreboding is proved to be false. For this, however, we will have to discard all the old prejudices in which even today we still indulge with such extreme pleasure—prejudices that are completely out of date. It is far more important to take up what is new.

Anyone with insight will know where the spirit is being sought, and there he will find assurance of future security. Where there is no search for the spirit there will be no hope for the future—for conquered or conqueror. Let one part of the world population demand milliards from another part, and the milliards will become melted gold that burns and destroys—while poverty, if given wings by the spirit, can carry men to heights that lead to the future evolution of humanity.

But this must be experienced by insight into the path of the spirit. No leaning toward anything external, no worshiping of new idols that are even now being made ready, can save mankind: only keeping to the spirit, holding fast to the spirit, working in the spirit.

Notes

1. Nikolaus von der Flue: 1417-1487. Urged arbitration as a method for resolving disputes.
2. Angelus Silesius: 1624-1677. See Rudolf Steiner, *Mysticism at the Dawn of the Modern Age*, GA 7 (Blauvelt, New York, Steinerbooks, 1980).
3. Rudolf Steiner, Dornach, 20 Dec. 1918, *Die Soziale Grundforderung unserer Zeit/in Geanderter Zeitlage*, GA 186 (Dornach, Rudolf Steiner Verlag, 1979).
4. World War I.
5. Rudolf Steiner, Dornach, 11 Jan. 1918, *Ancient Myths, Their Meaning and Connection with Evolution*, GA 180 (Vancouver, Steiner Book Centre, 1971).
6. David Lloyd-George: 1863-1945. British statesman. Elected to Parliament 1890; Prime Minister during World War I. One of the "Big Four" statesmen at Paris Peace Conference 1919.
7. Gnosis: esoteric knowledge in Greco-Latin world of the 2nd century A.D.
8. Waldenses and Cathars: heretical Christian sects in western Europe, 12th and 13th centuries. They joined the Reformation movement during the 16th century.
9. Manes: 216-274 A.D. See Rudolf Steiner, Nürnberg, 25 June 1908, *Apocalypse of St. John*, GA 104 (London, Rudolf Steiner Press, 1977).
10. Augustine: 354-430 A.D. See Rudolf Steiner, Dornach, 22 May 1920, *The Redemption of Thinking*, GA 74 (Spring Valley, Anthroposophic Press, 1983).
11. Scotus Erigena: 810-877 A.D. See Rudolf Steiner, *Riddles of Philosophy*, GA 18 (Spring Valley, Anthroposophic Press, 1973).

12. Jacob Boehme: 1575-1624 A.D. See Rudolf Steiner, *Mysticism at the Dawn of the Modern Age*, GA 7 (Blauvelt, NY, Steinerbooks, 1980).

13. Rudolf Steiner, *Christ in the Spiritual World and the Search for the Holy Grail*, GA 149 (London, Rudolf Steiner Press, 1963).

14. Council of Constantinople: 869 A.D. See Rudolf Steiner, *Building Stones for an Understanding of the Mystery of Golgotha*, GA 175 (London, Rudolf Steiner Press, 1972).

15. "which then was the beginning of the spiritual earth-world": original German, "die dann die geistige Erdenwelt ist."

16. Rudolf Steiner, 29 Nov. 1921, *Jesus oder Christus* (Dornach, Rudolf Steiner Verlag, 1980). Not translated.

17. Brunetto Latini: 1220-1294 A.D. See Rudolf Steiner, 13 July 1924, *Karmic Relationships Vol. III*, GA 236 (London, Rudolf Steiner Press, 1977)

18. Rudolf Steiner, *Ways to a New Style of Architecture*, GA 161 (New York, Anthroposophic Press, 1927).

19. Joachim and Boaz: from "Jachin" and "Boaz," words inscribed on the two columns at the front of Solomon's Temple. See the Old Testament, I Kings, Chapter 7; II Chronicles, Chap. 3; and Rudolf Steiner, *Bilder Okkulter Siegel und Saülen*, GA 284/285 (Dornach, Rudolf Steiner Verlag, 1977).

20. Walther Rathenau: 1867-1922. *Zürcher Zeitung*, Dec. 28, 1918.

21. Cardinal Newman: England, 1801-1890. Led Oxford movement in the Church of England. 1845, investment in Roman Catholic Church; became cardinal-deacon.

22. Rudolf Steiner, *Gospel of St. John, Gospel of St. John and Its Relation to the Other Gospels* (Spring Valley, Anthroposophic Press, 1984 and 1982).

FOR FURTHER READING

Rudolf Steiner intended these carefully written volumes to serve as a foundation to all of the later, more advanced anthroposophical writings and lecture courses.

THE PHILOSOPHY OF SPIRITUAL ACTIVITY by Rudolf Steiner. "Is human action free?" asks Steiner in his most important philosophical work. By first addressing the nature of knowledge, Steiner cuts across the ancient debate of real or illusory human freedom. A painstaking examination of human experience as a polarity of percepts and concepts shows that only in thinking does one escape the compulsion of natural law. Steiner's argument arrives at the recognition of the self-sustaining, universal reality of thinking that embraces both subjective and objective validity. Free acts can be performed out of love for a "moral intuition" grasped ever anew by a living thinking activity. Steiner scrutinizes numerous world-views and philosophical positions and finally indicates the relevance of his conclusion to human relations and life's ultimate questions. (262 pp)   Paper, $8.95 #1074; Cloth, $18.00 #1073

KNOWLEDGE OF THE HIGHER WORLDS AND ITS ATTAINMENT by Rudolf Steiner. Rudolf Steiner's fundamental work on the path to higher knowledge explains in detail the exercises and disciplines a student must pursue in order to attain a wakeful experience of supersensible realities. The stages of Preparation, Enlightenment, and Initiation are described, as is the transformation of dream-life and the meeting with the Guardian of the Threshold. Moral exercises for developing each of the spiritual lotus petal organs ("chakras") are given in accordance with the rule of taking three steps in moral development for each step into spiritual knowledge. The path described here is a safe one which will not interfere with the student's ability to lead a normal outer life. (272 pp)   Paper, $6.95 #80; Cloth, $14.00 #363

THEOSOPHY, AN INTRODUCTION TO THE SUPERSENSIBLE KNOWLEDGE OF THE WORLD AND THE DESTINATION OF MAN by Rudolf Steiner. In this work Steiner carefully explains many of the basic concepts and terminologies of anthroposophy. The book begins with a sensitive description of the primordial trichotomy: body, soul, and spirit, elaborating the various higher members of the human constitution. A discussion of reincarnation and karma follows. The next and longest chapter presents, in a vast panorama, the seven regions of the soul world, the seven regions of the land of spirits, and the soul's journey after death through these worlds. A brief discussion of the path to higher knowledge follows. (195 pp)   Paper, $6.95 #155; Cloth, $9.95 #154

AN OUTLINE OF OCCULT SCIENCE by Rudolf Steiner. This work begins with a thorough discussion and definition of the term "occult" science. A description of the supersensible nature of the human being follows, along with a discussion of dreams, sleep, death, life between death and rebirth, and reincarnation. In the fourth chapter evolution is described from the perspective of initiation science. The fifth chapter characterizes the training a student must undertake as a preparation for initiation. The sixth and seventh chapters consider the future evolution of the world and more detailed observations regarding supersensible realities. (388 pp)   Paper, $9.95 #113, Cloth, $16.00 #112

To order send a check including $2 for postage and handling (NY State residence please add local sales tax) to Anthroposophic Press, Bells Pond, Star Route, Hudson, NY 12534. Credit Card phone orders are accepted (518) 851-2054. (Prices subject to change)

A catalogue of over 300 titles is free on request.